My recipe keeper

My recipe keeper

Love Food ® is an imprint of Parragon Books Ltd

Parragon
Queen Street House
4 Queen Street
Bath BA1 1HE, UK

ISBN: 978-1-4075-2448-1

Printed in China

Designed by Lexi L'Esteve and Tom Cole
Edited by Fiona Biggs

Notes for the Reader
This book uses imperial, metric, and US cup
measurements. Follow the same units of
measurement throughout; do not mix metric
and imperial. All spoon measurements are
level: teaspoons are assumed to be 5 ml, and
tablespoons are assumed to be 15 ml. Unless
otherwise stated, milk is assumed to be whole,
eggs and individual vegetables are medium, and
pepper is freshly ground black pepper.
The times given are an approximate guide
only. Preparation times differ according to the
techniques used by different people and the
cooking times may also vary from those given.
Optional ingredients, variations, or serving
suggestions have not been included in the
calculations.
Recipes using raw or very lightly cooked eggs
should be avoided by infants, the elderly, pregnant
women, convalescents, and anyone with a chronic
condition. Pregnant and breastfeeding women
are advised to avoid eating peanuts and peanut
products. People with nut allergies should be
aware that some of the ready-prepared ingredients
used in the recipes in this book may contain nuts.
Always check the packaging before use.

Picture acknowledgments
Front cover: Cooking untensils—Image by
© J. Riou/photocuisine/Corbis
Images on pages 2 and 6 supplied courtesy of
Getty Images.

Contents

Chapter Content

Hints, tips & basic recipes

Essential kitchen equipment

Pastry boards

These are not always necessary if you have good kitchen counters. However, traditionally a large board made from wood was used to knead dough. It was also traditional to have a piece of marble on which to roll out pastry because of its cool qualities and its smooth surface, which allows the pastry to be moved around easily. If you are going to make pastry on a regular basis, it would be a sound investment to buy a specific board.

Rolling pins

In order to roll pastry well you need a heavy, smooth rolling pin. In emergencies a bottle can be used but it does not give an even rolling. Make sure the pin is of adequate length and has a smooth finish. Pins can be bought in a variety of materials: wood is traditional but you can buy metal and glass, which are cooler. Ceramic rolling pins used to be popular but seem to have gone out of fashion now. Rolling pins with handles have also become unpopular because they reduce the surface for rolling.

Pastry brushes

These brushes are useful for all kinds of jobs in the kitchen, such as brushing excess flour from the pastry and for glazing with egg or milk. They are also used for greasing pans and brushing oil on meat and poultry before and during cooking.

They are available in all shapes and sizes and in various materials. Wood is traditional but plastic brushes are now available—make sure you wash and dry them well or the bristles will start to fall out. Paint brushes are often used these days because they have a broad, flat brush, which covers the surface well. It is a good idea to have a very small one and a larger one for different tasks.

Pie weights

For years dried beans or rice have been used to weigh down wax paper or baking foil. This technique is known as "baking blind," and enables you to cook pastry without a filling until it is crisp; the filling is then added later. Today you can buy ceramic and aluminum "beans," which have a good weight and will last forever.

Cookie and baking sheets

A good, heavyweight cookie sheet is a must. It is not worth buying a cheap sheet because it will buckle in the oven and possibly spill the contents. Large cookie sheets should have only one upturned edge so that you can slip a large or delicate item on and off easily. Baking sheets with an edge all around are especially useful when making items such as sausage rolls, because they prevent the fat from spilling into the oven. Make sure the sheets are not too big for the oven—leave a gap all

around in order for the air to circulate properly.

Cake pans

You need to decide what types of cake you are interested in making because there are so many shapes and sizes of pan available. Perhaps the best starting point is two 8-inch/20-cm layer pans, at least 1 inch/2.5 cm deep. They can be used for both sponge cakes and layer cakes. When making bread use a 9 x 5 x 3-inch/23 x 13 x 8-cm loaf pan and two 8 x 4 x 2-inch/ 20 x 10 x 5-cm loaf pans at the same time (it does not seem worth making a smaller amount of dough or having the oven on for less). They can also be used individually for quick breads and fruit terrines. Always buy the best quality you can afford. Nonstick can be helpful but they still require a light coating of oil. Make sure you wash and dry them well before storing.

Muffins

A set of 12 mini-muffin pans or a regular muffin pan will be useful for making small cakes, tarts, and muffins, and for individual pies. If you are planning to bake quite frequently, or if you like to make batches of small fruit pies for parties, you will find a second pan helpful—you can assemble a second batch while the first batch is in the oven, making for more efficient working.

Quiche pans

Quiche pans or tart pans, call them what you will, these items are very useful for sweet and savory dishes. Always use steel pans, because those made from porcelain or glass do not allow the food to cook properly. Loose-bottom pans are the best because they allow you to remove the pan easily before serving; this is done by placing the flan on an upturned bowl and allowing the ring to fall to the surface. You can then transfer the flan on the bottom to a serving plate. An 8-inch/20-cm quiche pan is the most useful size, but if you have a large family or frequently cook for six or more people, a 12-inch/30-cm pan would be helpful. Small, individual pans are also available and these can be used for brown bag lunches or picnics.

Pie plates

Pie plates need to be quite deep with a good rim so that the pastry will be supported. They come in a number of sizes, usually oval or round, and can be glazed ceramic or glass. Some are made from enamel and tend to be oblong in shape. Larger ones need to be used with a pie funnel to support the pastry in the center.

Wire rack

A wire rack is particularly useful if you intend to bake bread and cakes. A rack allows the steam to escape from the baked items and prevents them from becoming too soggy. As soon as a cake is baked, turn it out of the pan onto an oven mitt-protected hand and then place it, bottom down, on the wire rack. This way the attractive crust on the top is maintained. Wire racks can usually be bought in rectangular or circular shapes.

Flour strainer or sieve

Sifting flour is important, not only to make sure there are no lumps but also to introduce air. A stainless steel strainer is best, of a medium size. It can also be used to strain vegetables, but make sure it is always cleaned and well dried after use. Plastic versions are also available. A very small strainer is useful for sprinkling confectioners' sugar over cakes and desserts, or you could use a tea strainer.

Flour sifter

A flour sifter makes it easier to sift flour onto pastry boards, dough, and rolling pins because it controls the amount of flour you use. I also find it useful for sprinkling flour into casseroles to prevent lumps from forming.

Mixing bowls

These bowls are available in stainless steel, copper, glass, plastic, and glazed ceramic. The choice is up to you. A large plastic bowl with a rubber base is particularly good, because the rubber base keeps the bowl steady when mixing. A metal bowl is good for whisking egg whites because it keeps cool and the surface can be kept absolutely smooth and clean. You will need a variety of sizes for different tasks, such as beating eggs and whipping cream. A selection of small bowls is ideal for assembling your prepared ingredients before starting to cook. Some come with lids, which is an added advantage.

Substitute ingredients

If you have decided to cook a recipe and discover that you don't have a particular ingredient, all is not lost. Use this list to discover if there is a way to substitute the item with a pantry standby.

If you need:	Quantity	Substitute:
Anchovies	1 fillet	$1/2$ tsp anchovy paste
Baking powder	1 tsp	$1/4$ tsp baking soda plus 1 tsp cream of tartar
Breadcrumbs, dried	1 cup	$3/4$ cup cracker crumbs
Broth, chicken or beef	1 cup	1 bouillon cube/1 tsp bouillon granules, dissolved in 1 cup boiling water
Butter	1 cup	1 cup margarine/$7/8$ cup vegetable oil, lard, or vegetable shortening/$4/5$ cup strained bacon fat/$3/4$ cup chicken fat
Cornstarch	1 tbsp	$2^{1}/_{2}$ tsp arrowroot or potato starch/5 tsp rice starch
Corn syrup, dark	1 cup	$3/4$ cup light corn syrup, plus $1/2$ cup molasses
Cream, light	1 cup	3 tbsp melted butter, made up to 1 cup with whole milk (for cooking and baking only)
Eggs	1 large	2 egg yolks plus 1 tbsp cold water/$3^{1}/_{2}$ tbsp refrigerated or frozen egg product, thawed/$2^{1}/_{2}$ tbsp each powdered whole egg and water
Flour, cake	1 cup	1 cup minus 2 tbsp all-purpose flour
Flour, self-rising	1 cup	1 cup all-purpose flour plus 1 tsp baking powder, $1/2$ tsp salt, and $1/4$ tsp baking soda
Garlic	1 small clove	$1/8$ tsp garlic powder/$1/2$ tsp bottled garlic
Ginger, fresh	1 tbsp chopped	$1/8$ tsp powdered ginger
Herbs, fresh	1 tsp snipped	1 tsp dried/$3/4$ tsp ground
Honey	1 cup	$1^{1}/_{4}$ cups granulated sugar plus $1/3$ cup of the liquid called for in the recipe
Lemon juice	1 tsp	$1/2$ tsp vinegar
Milk		
whole	1 cup	1 cup skim milk plus 2 tbsp melted butter or margarine
sour or buttermilk	1 cup	1 cup plain yogurt
Mustard, prepared	1 tbsp	1 tsp dry mustard
Onion	1 small, chopped	1 tbsp instant minced
Sour cream	1 cup	1 cup plain yogurt
Tomato juice	1 cup	$1/2$ cup tomato sauce plus $1/2$ cup water
Tomato ketchup	$1/2$ cup	$1/2$ cup tomato sauce plus 2 tbsp sugar and 1 tbsp vinegar
Tomato sauce	1 cup	$1/2$ cup tomato paste and $1/2$ cup water
Vanilla extract	1 tsp	1-inch/2.5-cm piece of vanilla bean
Vinegar		
balsamic	1 tbsp	1 tbsp red wine vinegar plus $1/2$ tsp light brown sugar
wine	1 tsp	2 tsp lemon juice
Yogurt	1 cup	1 cup buttermilk or 1 cup milk plus 1 tbsp lemon juice

Equivalents

Sometimes it's difficult to know what the quantity specified in a recipe means in real terms; for example 1 cup white rice will provide 3 cups cooked. Use this ready reckoner to establish how much of any ingredient you will need.

Food	Size or quantity	Equivalent
Apples	1lb/450 g fresh	3 medium/$2^3/_4$ cups chopped/3 cups sliced
	1 medium	$^2/_3$ cup chopped/1 cup sliced
Asparagus	1 lb/450 g fresh	12–20 spears/$3^1/_2$ cups chopped
Avocados	1 lb/450 g	$2^1/_2$ cups chopped/$1^1/_2$ cups puréed
Breadcrumbs	$^1/_2$ cup fresh	1 slice bread
	$^1/_2$ cup dried	1 slice toast
Butter/margarine	1 lb/450 g	2 cups/4 sticks
Cheese		
cheddar	1 lb/450 g	4 cups grated
Parmesan	1 lb/450 g	4 cups grated
Ginger, fresh	2-inch/5-cm piece	2 tsp minced
Lemons	1 medium	3 tbsp juice/2–3 tsp zest
Limes	1 medium	1–2 tbsp juice/1 tsp zest
Meat, ground	1 lb/450 g	2 cups uncooked
Mushrooms	1 lb/450 g fresh	5 cups sliced/6 cups chopped
	3 oz dried	1 lb/450 g reconstituted
Mussels	1 lb/450 g	20 medium
Onions	1 lb/450 g	4 medium
Peppers, bell	1 lb/450 g	2 large/$2^1/_2$ cups chopped/3 cups sliced
Rice	1 cup white	3 cups cooked
	1 cup brown	$3^1/_2$–4 cups cooked
Shrimp	1 lb/450 g peeled	8 oz/225 g meat/2 cups cooked meat
Tomatoes	1 lb/450 g fresh	3 medium/$1^1/_2$ cups chopped/2 cups sliced
	14 oz/425 g canned	$1^1/_3$ cups including juice
Yogurt	8 fl oz/225 ml	1 cup/$^1/_2$ pint

Oven temperatures

Fahrenheit	Celsius	Oven Heat
225°	110°	very cool
250°	120°	very cool
275°	140°	cool
300°	150°	cool
325°	160°	moderate
350°	180°	moderate
375 °	190°	moderately hot
400°	200°	moderately hot
425°	220°	hot
450°	230°	very hot

Spoon measurements

1 teaspoon of liquid = 5 ml

1 tablespoon of liquid = 15 ml

Other measurements

Liquid volume	
U.S. standard	Metric
2 fl oz	50 ml
$3^1/_2$ fl oz	100 ml
4 fl oz	125 ml
$^1/_2$ cup	125 m
5 fl oz	150 m
7 fl oz	200 ml
8 fl oz	225 ml
1 cup	225 ml
10 fl oz	300 m
16 fl oz	475 ml
18 fl oz	525 ml
$2^1/_2$ cups	700 ml
3 cups	850 ml
4 cups	1.5 litres

Weight	
Imperial	Metric
$^1/_8$ oz	5 g
$^1/_4$ oz	10 g
1 oz	25 g
2 oz	55 g
$2^3/_4$ oz	75 g
3 oz	85 g
$3^1/_2$ oz	100 g
$5^1/_2$ oz	150 g
8 oz	225 g
$10^1/_2$ oz	300 g
1 lb	450 g
1lb 2 oz	500 g
2 lb 4 oz	1 kg
3 lb 5 oz	1.5 kg

Cooking methods

Baking

This is the term used for cooking food in the oven by dry heat, for example, a baked potato or baked custard. It is also the process for preparing baked goods, such as cakes, cookies, and bread.

Basting

The process of moistening meat, fish, or poultry while roasting in the oven. The cooking juices and fat are spooned over the food to keep it moist, to add flavor, and to improve the appearance of the finished dish. If the pan becomes too dry, then a little liquid, either stock or wine, can be added to the juices. Roasting vegetables are basted with oil so that they are well coated and will crisp evenly, and fried eggs can be basted with hot oil to make sure the tops of the eggs are set.

Blanching

Blanching used to mean "to whiten" and was used to whiten veal and variety meats. Today there are two more usual meanings. The first is to immerse food in boiling water for a few seconds and then into cold water in order to remove their skins. The other is in preparing vegetables for freezing by immersing the vegetables in boiling water for a short period to destroy enzymes that will spoil the flavor and texture, and then into cold water to stop the cooking process. Blanching also helps to preserve the color of vegetables.

Boiling

This is cooking food in a liquid (water, stock, or milk) at 212°F/100°C (known as boiling point). The main foods cooked in this way are eggs, vegetables, rice, and pasta. Although sometimes fish and meat are placed in boiling liquids, the heat is then reduced, and the food is simmered only. Continued boiling would render these foods lacking in flavor, shrunken in size, and of poor texture.

Braising

A long, slow, moist method of cooking used for cuts of meat, poultry, and game that are too tough to roast. Braised food is usually cooked in one piece and the amount of liquid used is very small. The food is browned in oil and then cooked with vegetables in a casserole with a close-fitting lid. The dish can then be cooked either on the stove top or in a low oven.

Broiling

A very quick and easy method of cooking, which is also very healthy. The food is cooked by radiant heat, which makes sure that the outside of the food is well cooked and browned while the inside remains moist. The food must be tender and of good quality, for example steak, chops, chicken, burgers, sausages, whole fish such as trout, and cutlets and fillets of salmon and cod. Vegetables, such as mushrooms, bell peppers, tomatoes, and onions, are also suitable for broiling. The broiler must be preheated and the food brushed with oil to give a little protection from the fierce heat. Cooking on the barbecue is the outdoor equivalent of broiling and is suitable for all the above foods although it produces a more smoky flavor.

Casseroling

Another, more modern name for braising, taken from the name of the cooking vessel—an ovenproof casserole dish with a tight-fitting lid (this is often flameproof and can be used for the initial browning process, which cuts down on the dish washing). The food is often served from the casserole dish at the table. Casseroling also includes stews, in which the pieces of food are often cut into small pieces and more liquid is used.

Frying

The process of cooking food in hot fat. There are three main ways to fry food: pan-frying or sautéing, shallow-fat frying, and deep-fat frying. Frying gives the food a delicious golden-brown color and a wonderful flavor.

Pan-frying

A more modern method of cooking, pan-frying is devised to cook food quickly and easily in a healthier way that uses very little fat. Some naturally fatty foods, such as bacon and sausages, can be dry-fried because they contain enough of their own fat to be sure that they will not burn. Small cuts of meat, poultry, and fish are cooked at a high temperature in a very little fat (half vegetable oil and half butter are ideal for this because the oil allows the fat to reach a high temperature without burning and the butter adds the flavor). The food is added to the hot skillet, either with or without a little hot fat, and cooked on one side; the heat quickly seals the food and keeps it moist and tender. It is then turned over and cooked on the other side until cooked through. The food is then removed from the skillet to a warm plate and a sauce can be made with the cooking juices and a dash of wine or stock. Pan-fried food is served immediately.

Shallow-fat frying

This method is used for coated foods, for example fish cakes and crumbed fish, or scallops of meat and chicken, which are coated with flour or breadcrumbs. Use a vegetable oil, such as corn oil, in a shallow skillet and allow enough oil to prevent the food from sticking. The thicker the food, the more oil you will need. Heat the skillet and the oil to a high temperature and add the food: the oil will seal the food and will not allow it to absorb too much fat. Once cooked on one side, turn the food over and cook on the other side. Remove it from the skillet with a metal spatula or a slotted spoon, shake it gently to remove excess oil, and drain on paper towels, which will absorb any remaining fat. Serve while still hot.

Deep-fat frying

With this method, food is cooked while completely immersed in hot fat. The choice of fat is important because you need an oil that can be heated to a high temperature without smoking. Corn oil and soybean oil both have high smoke points—in other words, they smoke at a higher temperature—and are good for deep-frying. However, peanut oil is the best; it has one of the highest smoke points.

Foods need a protective coating when they are deep-fried and popular coverings are breadcrumbs or batter. The most usual foods to deep-fry are French fries, shellfish, fish, and chicken. For this method, you need a deep, heavy pan and a wire basket to lift the food

out. It is a dangerous method of cooking because a very high temperature is needed and many fires in the home are caused by deep-fat pans catching fire. A better method is to have an electric deep-fryer, which is thermostatically controlled so it is safer and easier to use.

Griddling

A griddle was once a flat metal plate used on the stove top to cook cakes and cookies. Nowadays, the expression "to griddle" refers to a ridged grill pan similar to a skillet—it has a ridged surface, which gives the food attractive brown stripes. This equipment has become popular because it is used by many television chefs. It does produce very appetizing food and is a healthy way of cooking because the food needs only a light brushing of oil. Griddling is suitable for thin steaks, chicken, salmon fillets, squid and shellfish, and for vegetables such as eggplant, zucchini, bell peppers, fennel, and onions.

Poaching

A gentle method of cooking food in a liquid at simmering point (see Simmering, below). Poaching is suitable for small pieces of fish, for example steaks or fillets, particularly for smoked fish such as haddock and cod because the liquid absorbs some of the flavor and can then be used to make a sauce. Whole chickens can be poached so that the meat is succulent and tender and the well-flavored stock can be used for soups. Whole fish such as salmon can be poached to serve whole. Poached eggs are simple to cook if you use very fresh eggs. Fruit also lends itself to poaching because the long, slow cooking

tenderizes the fruit without losing its shape and you have a well-flavored juice to serve with it.

Simmering

A method of cooking in liquid like boiling, but simmering is done at a lower temperature, just below boiling point. It is easy to control because you can judge it by eye. Boiling liquid has large bubbles and the surface is very agitated, but liquid at simmering point has just a gentle stream of small bubbles hardly breaking the surface. The simmering method is suitable for vegetables, chicken, fish, and fruit.

Steaming

This technique involves cooking food in the steam of boiling water, either in direct contact or indirectly. Steaming is an economical method of cooking because more than one item can be cooked at a time. It is also a healthy method of cooking because there is no immersion in water and therefore very little loss of nutrients.

The most usual foods to be cooked by steaming are vegetables; often potatoes are boiled in a pan and a steamer is set over the top and other vegetables cooked in the steam. You can buy 1–2-tiered steamers, which will fit over your pan and enable you to cook more than one vegetable at a time. The firmer vegetable should be in the bottom of the steamer and the more tender one at the top (where it is slightly cooler). The whole steamer is covered with a lid until the vegetables are tender.

Bamboo steamers are now very popular and inexpensive. They can be used for fish, poultry, and vegetables. Just bring a small amount of water to a boil in a pan or a wok and stack up the steamers containing the food.

Another type of steamer is the small, folding metal steamer. It is small and so not very difficult to store and will fit inside any pan. Bring 1 inch/2.5 cm of water to a boil in a pan and place the steamer and the vegetables in the pan, cover with the pan lid, and steam until they are tender.

Steaming is also used for desserts. The dessert bowl, well covered, is placed in the pan, on a trivet if you have one. The pan is filled halfway up with boiling water and the dessert is steamed for the correct length of time, checking the water level from time to time. Steaming produces a lighter, softer dessert than one that is baked.

Roasting

This is a method of cooking food in the oven, like baking, but it is usually used for meat, poultry, and vegetables (nowadays we roast fish as well). Roasting often requires added fat to protect the food and moisten it while it is cooked at a relatively high temperature. Roasted meats are cooked in a fairly shallow roasting pan to allow the air to circulate and the surface of the meat to brown. Large, tender cuts of meat and tender poultry and game are suitable for roasting. If you are in any doubt about the tenderness of the meat, braise or casserole it instead. The cooking juices can be used to make a gravy to accompany the meat.

The most popular roast vegetable is the potato, but we can now roast all kinds of vegetables—parsnips, squashes, turnips, fennel, onions, garlic, carrots, sweet potatoes, tomatoes, bell peppers, and eggplant—giving them a delicious and intense flavor.

Sautéing

This method is similar to frying, but sautéing usually means "moving" the food at the same time. The most common use of this method is preparing onions for stews or casseroles. The onions are fried in a little oil in a skillet (or a sauté pan, which is slightly deeper) but you keep them moving because they are finely chopped and need to be kept moving to prevent them from burning in the hot skillet or pan. It is this technique that has evolved as stir-frying.

Stewing

This long, slow method of cooking is very like braising, that is to say, cooking in a liquid. It is used for tougher cuts of meat, older chickens, and game. In a stew the meat is usually cut up into small pieces and cooked in a large quantity of liquid. The liquid usually needs to be thickened or reduced before serving with the meat. Stewed fruit is often still referred to, but often the term "poached" is now used instead. This is particularly so when the fruit is left whole, as in poached peaches. However, the term "stewed apple" is still used to describe fruit that has been broken down to form a purée.

Stir-frying

This is a very quick way of cooking small pieces of food in a healthy and appetizing way. It has become a very popular way to cook because it is seen regularly on television programs and also the availability of woks has become widespread. Stir-frying means sautéing a variety of foods together at a high temperature. In order to achieve this, you need to prepare the meat or fish and the vegetables in advance. Make sure all the pieces are the same size so that they will cook evenly. If you do not have a wok, a large skillet will suffice. Make sure everything is prepared before you start to cook because it takes very little time once started. Heat a little oil in the pan and make sure it is really hot before cooking. Cook only small quantities at a time because you need the food to fry and not to steam. In fact, stir-frying should really be done for only one or two people at a time—any more and some of you will not have fresh, hot food.

The most successful foods cooked in this way are thin strips of beef or pork, strips of chicken breast portions, shrimp, scallops, slices of salmon, flounder, or monkfish, and plenty of vegetables that are popular in Chinese cooking, such as beansprouts, bok choy, Chinese cabbage, cabbage, mushrooms, bell peppers, and scallions. Noodles are often added toward the end of the cooking time. Since this method of cooking mainly comes from Asia, suitable flavors are also added, for example ginger, soy sauce, and sesame oil.

Basic nutrition

Sensible, healthy eating requires a good balance of food. A diet that contains carbohydrates, fats, protein, vitamins, and minerals, plus plenty of fiber and water, will ensure that the body continues to function correctly.

Carbohydrates
This group includes all sugars, starches, and fiber. Sugars are referred to as simple carbohydrates because they have a simple structure and can be broken down by the body easily to give a rush of instant energy. Too much sugar, however, can increase the risk of diabetes, heart disease, obesity, and tooth decay.
Complex carbohydrates are present in whole grains such as corn, oats, and barley and in fresh fruit and vegetables. Their complex structure takes longer to break down in the body and provides a longer, steadier flow of energy in the bloodstream.

Fiber
Fiber cannot be digested, but it is still very important in the diet because it provides bulk to assist the passage of the food through the intestines. Maintaining a good intake of fiber helps to prevent constipation.

Protein
Protein is essential for growth and repair of the body, and any excess can be used to provide energy. Proteins have a complex structure and are composed of amino acids. The ones that are necessary for the human body are called essential amino acids. These are present in the correct ratio in animal proteins and are said to have a high biological value. Vegetable proteins, known as incomplete proteins, provide only some of the essential amino acids and therefore need to be eaten in combinations that complement each other in order to provide the correct balance of amino acids.

Fats
Oils and fats are present in the diet as the most concentrated form of energy. They are available as visible fats, such as butter, margarine, oils, and fat on meat, but also as invisible fat in cheese, cookies, cakes, chips, and nuts. Not all fats are bad. The baddies are the saturated fatty acids found in animal fats such as butter and cheese and in animal products such as sausages, bacon, pork, lamb, hamburgers, eggs, and whole milk. Saturated fats are thought to increase blood cholesterol levels and therefore to be responsible for heart disease. Polyunsaturated and monounsaturated fatty acids, on the other hand, are believed to reduce cholesterol levels; these are available in corn oil, olive oil, soy, and sunflower oils, and nut oils (but not coconut).

Vitamins
Vitamins help to regulate important body processes. Apart from vitamin D, all the vitamins must be supplied in the diet because the body is unable to manufacture them.
Vitamins are either water-soluble or fat-soluble. Water-soluble vitamins include vitamins B_1, B_2, B_6, and B_{12} and vitamin C; the fat-soluble vitamins include A, D, E, and K. Vitamins may be taken as supplements, but they are expensive, and if you have a well-balanced diet they should be unnecessary.

Minerals
Minerals are inorganic elements needed by the body in very small amounts. Calcium, phosphorus, and magnesium are important constituents of bones and teeth. Sodium, chloride, magnesium, potassium, and phosphorus are present as soluble salts in body fluids. Iron, phosphorus, and zinc aid the process of releasing energy. Trace elements, such as copper, fluoride, selenium, iodine, manganese, chromium, and cobalt, are also needed, but in smaller amounts. A well-balanced diet should provide all of these elements. Supplements are widely available but they should always be used with discretion.

Water
The most essential part of any diet is to drink at least eight 8-fl oz/225-ml glasses of water every day. Water is needed in the body for transporting nutrients, for digestion, for circulation, for body heat regulation, and for excretion. No matter how healthy your diet, if you are not drinking enough water, your body will not function properly and you will feel lethargic and sluggish.

Preparation techniques

Baking blind

This means baking pastry shells without a filling so that the pastry is well cooked and crisp. The quiche pan or pie dish is lined with pie dough or sweet pastry and then lined with parchment paper or foil, which is then weighed down with baking beans (these can be dried beans or ceramic or metal ones) to prevent the pastry from bubbling up while cooking. The beans and foil are then removed and the pie shell cooked for a while longer to dry it thoroughly.

Beating

This term refers to mixing food to make it lighter by incorporating air. You can use a fork, a wooden spoon, or an electric mixer for beating. It is most often used for eggs, for an omelet, and for making a cake, beating together the butter and sugar (this is also known as creaming). It is also used to beat a sauce or a custard, not to incorporate air but to make the consistency smooth and remove any lumps.

Blending

Blending means combining ingredients together, usually with a spoon. You can blend cornstarch and water, for example, to a smooth paste before using to thicken soups and stews. Blending also refers to mixing soups and purées in a blender to reduce to a smooth liquid and remove any lumps.

Crimping

This means to decorate the edges of a pie in order to ensure the edges are well sealed. This is done by pinching the pastry with a finger and thumb of one hand and pressing with the first finger of the other hand, giving a fluted edge. Crimping is also used purely decoratively on shortbread or plate pies.

Cutting

Cutting is a basic technique used to prepare meat, fruit, and vegetables. Using a knife correctly is an important step in preparing food. Food that is correctly prepared will cook more evenly and have a more attractive appearance. A good knife and a firm board are essential. Make sure the knife is sharp because blunt knives cause accidents. Use the correct knife for the task, for example a bread knife for bread and a serrated knife for tomatoes.

Chopping

This is one step on from cutting. The food is divided into small pieces by more than one cut. To chop an onion, for example, you halve the onion from the top down through the stem and root, then you place the flat side of one half down on the board, and cut the onion from root to stem into fine slices. Then you turn the knife and slice through the onion the other way making sure that you have even pieces. Chopping herbs is another important skill. Hold the tip of the blade down with one hand and move the handle of the knife up and down with your other hand as you chop into the herb, moving from left to right and back again so that you work all over the food.

Chopping can be done roughly or finely: rough chopping produces pieces of food about 1/2 inch/1 cm, whereas fine chopping produces much smaller pieces. It is important to chop all the pieces to an even size. Sometimes a recipe might ask for food to be diced: this means pieces not only of the same size but of a regular shape; for example, diced cucumber should be small cubes.

Crushing

This technique is used for crushing herbs or garlic. To crush garlic, simply press down on the garlic using the flat side of a knife blade. Crushing is also used for making cookie crumbs for cheesecakes or flan shells. To make cookie crumbs, simply put the cookies in a large plastic bag, cover the end, and then crush with a rolling pin until they are reduced to crumbs. You can also crush garlic cloves with a garlic press or a heavy knife.

Dredging

Dredging means sprinkling dough with flour before rolling it out. The board and the rolling pin should be lightly floured to prevent the pastry from sticking. The term can also be used for sugar and unsweetened cocoa powder, as in dredging a cake with confectioners' sugar. These days it is fashionable to dredge a plate with sugar or cocoa powder before serving a dessert.

Folding in

The term used to describe how to incorporate flour into a cake mixture. It is a gentle movement, made with a metal spoon or a plastic spatula to cut through the mixture in a figure-eight movement, enabling the flour to combine without losing the air already incorporated. The same term applies to meringues and soufflés.

Glazing

A glaze is a finish given to pastry and bread before baking. It can be simply milk, or beaten egg, or a water and sugar glaze.

Grating

A grater is used to shred food into small particles. The two most common uses are for cheese and for citrus fruit peel. A box-shaped grater is useful because it has different-size surfaces and can produce medium and fine gratings. A food processor can grate food quickly and is useful if you have a large quantity to prepare.

Grinding

Grinding reduces foods to a powder or very small particles for use in recipes. For example, you can grind spices in a mortar with a pestle until you have achieved the required texture. A food processor will grind nuts and chocolate satisfactorily. Grinding also means chopping food, such as lean beef, pork, lamb, chicken, or turkey, very finely. It is best done with a hand or electric meat grinder. A food processor can also be used to grind food.

Kneading

This technique is used in breadmaking. The dough is kneaded to develop the gluten in the flour so that it will hold its shape when risen. The dough is pummeled on a lightly floured board until it is smooth and elastic. Kneading involves a particular technique that uses the heal of the hand to pull and stretch the dough, which can be therapeutic. Kneading can also be done in a free-standing mixer using a dough hook.

Marinating

This is soaking food in a marinade to tenderize it and add flavor. Marinating is used for meat, poultry, and game. The meat is covered with a mixture of oil, wine, or vinegar, and flavorings such garlic and herbs. The food can be marinated for a few hours or a few days. During cooking, the marinade can be used to baste the food.

Mashing

This usually refers to potatoes and other root vegetables. Cooked vegetables are mashed, using a fork, a potato masher, or an electric mixer. This makes them smooth and light and other flavors can be incorporated at the same time, for example, herbs, garlic, and mustard. The addition of butter or cream makes them more luxurious.

Punching down

This is the term for knocking the air out of the bread dough after its first rising and then gently kneading for 1 minute. The dough is then gently shaped before a second rising or "proving" in a warm place.

Rubbing in

This is a method of making cakes, pastry, and bread where the fat is rubbed into the flour using the tips of the fingers, lifting the flour high out of the bowl so that the air will be trapped in the mixture. This makes the mixture lighter.

Scoring

A method of making light cuts on the surface of food to help it cook more quickly, to reduce fat, and to make food look more attractive.

Straining

This is a method of rubbing cooked food through a strainer to form a purée. The food is pushed through the strainer using a wooden spoon. Straining can also refer to straining vegetables after cooking to remove the cooking water.

Sifting

This is the same as straining (see above) but refers to dry ingredients, for example sugar and flour, to remove lumps and to add air to the mixture. With these finer ingredients, however, there is no need to push them through with a wooden spoon.

Tenderizing

This is beating raw meat with a rolling pin or a meat mallet to soften the fibers and make the meat tender before frying or broiling.

Trussing

This is the technique used for poultry and game whereby the bird is pulled into shape and then held with skewers or by string to maintain its shape during cooking.

Whisking

This is another method used to incorporate air, but it is usually used for a lighter mixture, for example egg whites or cream. To make the task easier and more efficient, you really need an electric mixer for whisking. However, a wire whisk used in a large mixing bowl with plenty of energy can perform the task adequately. Indeed, many chefs prefer to use their wire whisks and a copper bowl for meringues.

Kitchen hygiene

Buying food

Always buy from a reputable source where you have confidence in their food handling techniques. Try to buy the freshest foods and the best quality possible.

Storing

Keep food for as short a time as possible before cooking or serving, and make sure that it is stored at a safe temperature.

A refrigerator should operate at below 41°F/5°C, so keep a thermometer in the refrigerator and check it from time to time to be sure it is working satisfactorily. Adjust the thermostat when necessary.

Cover all food in the refrigerator with plastic wrap so that one food will not contaminate another. Be specially careful of any meat products, which might leak blood onto other foods.

Check expiration dates on food packaging before cooking.

Thaw all frozen food thoroughly before cooking. Thaw it overnight in the refrigerator instead of at room temperature.

Preparing

Carefully wash any foods that need cleaning and dry well with paper towels—this is more hygienic than using a cloth.

Wash your own hands frequently with soap when preparing food. Use a separate hand towel, not a dish towel.

Keep counters clean and use different cutting boards for cooked and uncooked foods, particularly meats. Wash them well and then rinse with diluted bleach between each use. Wash knives and other kitchen utensils in hot water and soap between each use.

Keep dish cloths clean and make sure that you change them often. Keep trash cans covered and empty them frequently, disinfecting regularly.

Cooking

Make sure food is cooked thoroughly and is served piping hot as soon as is practicable.

When cooked food needs to be kept, make sure it is cooled quickly, covered, and placed in the refrigerator as soon as possible. It is when food is kept at room temperature that food-poisoning bacteria have an opportunity to multiply, so avoid keeping foods for long periods at this temperature.

Only reheat food once; if it is not then used up, throw it away. It is safer than risking illness. However, never reheat a marinade, especially one used for marinating meat.

Basic recipes

Vegetable stock

Makes about 8$\frac{1}{2}$ cups

2 tbsp sunflower or corn oil

scant $\frac{1}{2}$ cup finely chopped onion

scant $\frac{1}{2}$ cup finely chopped leek

$\frac{2}{3}$ cup finely chopped carrots

4 celery stalks, finely chopped

$\frac{3}{4}$ cup finely chopped fennel

1 small tomato, finely chopped

10 cups water

1 bouquet garni

Heat the oil in a large pan. Add the onion and leek and cook over low heat, stirring occasionally, for 5 minutes, until softened. Add the remaining vegetables, cover, and cook for 10 minutes. Add the water and bouquet garni, bring to a boil, and simmer for 20 minutes.

Strain the stock into a bowl, let cool, cover, and store in the refrigerator. Use immediately or freeze in portions for up to 3 months.

Fish stock

Makes about 5$\frac{1}{4}$ cups

1 lb 7 oz/650 g white fish heads, bones, and trimmings, rinsed

1 onion, sliced

2 celery stalks, chopped

1 carrot, sliced

1 bay leaf

4 fresh parsley sprigs

4 black peppercorns

$\frac{1}{2}$ lemon, sliced

5$\frac{2}{3}$ cups water

$\frac{1}{2}$ cup dry white wine

Cut out and discard the gills from any fish heads, then place the heads, bones, and trimmings in a pan. Add all the remaining ingredients and gradually bring to a boil, skimming off the foam that rises to the surface. Partially cover and simmer for 25 minutes.

Strain the stock without pressing down on the contents of the sieve. Let cool, cover, and store in the refrigerator. Use immediately or freeze in portions for up to 3 months.

Chicken stock

Makes about 10 cups

  3 lb/1.3 kg chicken wings and necks

  2 onions, cut into wedges

  $17^1/_2$ cups water

  2 carrots, coarsely chopped

  2 celery stalks, coarsely chopped

  10 fresh parsley sprigs

  4 fresh thyme sprigs

  2 bay leaves

  10 black peppercorns

Put the chicken wings and necks and the onions in a large, heavy-bottom pan and cook over low heat, stirring frequently, until lightly browned.

Add the water and stir well to scrape off any sediment from the bottom of the pan. Gradually bring to a boil, skimming off the foam that rises to the surface. Add all the remaining ingredients, partially cover, and simmer for 3 hours.

Strain the stock into a bowl, let cool, cover, and store in the refrigerator. When cold, remove and discard the layer of fat from the surface. Use immediately or freeze in portions for up to 6 months.

Beef stock

Makes about $7^1/_2$ cups

  2 lb 4 oz/1 kg beef marrow bones, cut into
    3-inch/7.5-cm pieces

  1 lb 7 oz/650 g braising beef in a single piece

  $12^1/_2$ cups water

  4 cloves

  2 onions, halved

  2 celery stalks, coarsely chopped

  8 black peppercorns

  1 bouquet garni

Place the bones in the bottom of a large pan and put the meat on top. Add the water and gradually bring to a boil, skimming off the foam that rises to the surface.

Press a clove into each onion half and add to the pan with the celery, peppercorns, and bouquet garni. Partially cover and simmer for 3 hours. Remove the meat and simmer for 1 hour more.

Strain the stock into a bowl, let cool, cover, and store in the refrigerator. When cold, remove and discard the layer of fat from the surface. Use immediately or freeze in portions for up to 6 months.

Béchamel sauce

Makes about 1¹/₂ cups

1¹/₄ cups milk

1 small onion, studded with 2–3 cloves

1 mace blade

1 fresh bay leaf

3–4 white or black peppercorns

1 small piece of carrot, peeled

2 tbsp unsalted butter or margarine

¹/₄ cup all-purpose flour

salt and pepper

Pour the milk into a small heavy-bottom pan with a lid. Add the onion, mace, bay leaf, peppercorns, and carrot. Heat over gentle heat and slowly bring to just boiling point. Remove from the heat, cover, and set aside for at least 30 minutes. Strain and reheat until warm.

Melt the butter in a separate small pan and sprinkle in the flour. Cook over gentle heat, stirring continuously with a wooden spoon, for 2 minutes. Remove from the heat and gradually stir in the warmed infused milk, adding a little at a time and stirring until the milk has been incorporated before adding more. When all the milk has been added, return to the heat and cook, stirring, until thick, smooth, and glossy. Add salt and pepper to taste and serve.

Beurre blanc

Makes about ¹/₂ cup

2 tbsp finely chopped shallot

2 tbsp white wine vinegar

¹/₂ cup unsalted butter

salt and pepper

Put the shallot in a small heavy-bottom pan with the vinegar and salt and pepper to taste. Bring to a boil and boil for 2–3 minutes until reduced to about 2 teaspoons. Add 2 tablespoons of the butter and beat vigorously with a wire whisk while bringing to a boil. Remove from the heat and whisk in the remaining butter, a piece at a time. When all the butter has been added, check and adjust the seasoning if necessary, and serve.

Greek garlic sauce

Makes about 1 cup

1 cup whole blanched almonds

3 tbsp fresh white breadcrumbs

2 large garlic cloves, crushed

2 tsp lemon juice

$^2/_3$ cup extra virgin olive oil

4 tbsp hot water

salt and pepper

Put the almonds in a food processor and blend until finely ground. Add the breadcrumbs, garlic, lemon juice, and salt and pepper to taste, and mix well together. With the machine running, very slowly pour in the oil to form a smooth, thick mixture. When all the oil has been added, blend in the water. Turn the mixture into a bowl and chill for at least 2 hours.

Aïoli

Makes about 1$^1/_4$ cups

1 large egg yolk

1 tbsp white wine vinegar or lemon juice

2 large garlic cloves, peeled and crushed

5 tbsp extra virgin olive oil

5 tbsp sunflower oil

salt and pepper

Put the egg yolk, vinegar, garlic, and salt and pepper to taste in a bowl and whisk until all the ingredients are well blended. Add the olive oil, then the sunflower oil, drop by drop at first, and then in a slow, steady stream until thick and smooth.

Hollandaise sauce

Makes about 1 cup

2 tbsp white wine vinegar

1 tbsp water

2 egg yolks

$^1/_2$ cup unsalted butter, slightly softened and diced

lemon juice (optional)

salt and pepper

Pour the vinegar and water into a small heavy-bottom pan and bring to a boil. Boil for 3 minutes, or until reduced by half. Remove from the heat and let cool slightly.

Put the egg yolks in a heatproof bowl and beat in the cooled vinegar water. Set over a pan of gently simmering water, ensuring that the bottom of the bowl does not touch the simmering water. Cook, stirring continuously, until the mixture thickens slightly and lightly coats the back of the spoon. Keeping the water simmering, add the butter, a piece at a time, until the sauce is thick, smooth, and glossy. Add a little lemon juice, if using, and salt and pepper to taste and serve warm.

Tartare sauce

Makes about 1$\frac{1}{4}$ cups

2 large egg yolks

2 tsp Dijon mustard

2 tbsp lemon juice or white
wine vinegar

about 1$\frac{1}{4}$ cups sunflower oil

10 cornichons, finely chopped

1 tbsp capers, finely chopped

1 tbsp finely chopped parsley

salt and pepper

Whiz the egg yolks with the mustard, and pepper and salt
to taste, in a food processor or blender or by hand. Add the
lemon juice and whiz again. With the motor still running or
still beating, add the oil, drop by drop at first. When the sauce
begins to thicken, the oil can then be added in a slow, steady
stream. Stir in the cornichons, capers, and parsley. Taste and
adjust the seasoning with extra salt and pepper and lemon juice
if necessary. If the sauce seems too thick, slowly add
1 tablespoon of hot water. Use at once or store in an airtight
container in the refrigerator for up to 1 week.

Mayonnaise

Makes about 1$\frac{1}{4}$ cups

2 egg yolks

$\frac{2}{3}$ cup sunflower oil

$\frac{2}{3}$ cup olive oil

1 tbsp white wine vinegar

2 tsp Dijon mustard

salt and pepper

Beat the egg yolks with a pinch of salt. Combine the sunflower
oil and the olive oil in a pitcher. Gradually add one quarter of
the oil mixture to the beaten egg, a drop at a time, beating
continuously with a whisk or electric mixer. Beat in the vinegar,
then continue adding the combined oils in a steady stream,
beating continuously. Stir in the mustard and season with salt
and pepper to taste.

Slimline dressing

Makes about 1¼ cups

1¼ cups lowfat plain yogurt

1 tsp English mustard

2–3 tbsp lemon juice

4 tsp sunflower oil

salt and pepper

Put all the ingredients into a food processor, season with pepper and salt to taste, and process on medium speed until thoroughly combined.

Garlic, chile & oregano oil

Makes about 1 cup

5 garlic cloves, halved lengthwise

2 tbsp seeded and chopped red hot chile

1 tsp dried oregano

1 cup canola oil

Preheat the oven to 300°F/150°C. Combine the garlic, chile, and oregano with the oil in an ovenproof glass measuring cup. Place on a glass pie plate in the center of the oven and heat for 1½–2 hours. The temperature of the oil should reach 250°F/120°C.

Remove from the oven, let cool, then strain through cheesecloth into a clean jar. Store, covered, in the refrigerator. You can also leave the garlic and chile pieces in the oil and strain before using.

Tomato dressing

Makes ½ cup

2 tbsp balsamic vinegar, or red or white wine vinegar

4–6 tbsp extra virgin olive oil

1 tsp Dijon mustard

pinch of superfine sugar

1 tbsp torn fresh basil leaves

1 tbsp chopped sun-dried tomatoes

salt and pepper

Place all the ingredients in a screw-top jar, secure the top, and shake well. Alternatively, beat all the ingredients together in a small bowl. Use as much oil as you like.

If you have just salad greens to dress, 4 tablespoons of oil will be sufficient, but if you have heavier ingredients, such as potatoes, you will need about 6 tablespoons of oil.

Use the dressing at once. If you want to store it, do not add the herbs—it will then keep for 3–4 days in the refrigerator.

Basic dough recipe

The method used is basically the same for all yeast breads, although individual steps may vary according to the recipe.

Makes 1 loaf

> $4^1/_2$ cups white bread flour
>
> 2 tsp salt
>
> 2 tsp active dry yeast
>
> 2 cups lukewarm water
>
> 2 tbsp olive oil or butter

Sift the flour and salt into a large bowl. Stir in the yeast and make a well in the center. Pour in the liquid and mix to a soft, sticky dough.

Turn out the dough onto a lightly floured counter and begin kneading by folding the dough over on top of itself and pushing away with the heel of your hand—do not be afraid to be forceful. Keep kneading, giving the dough a quarter turn as you do so, for 10 minutes, or until the dough is very smooth and elastic and no longer sticky. Alternatively, knead the dough in an mixer, using a dough hook attachment, for 6–8 minutes.

Form the dough into a ball and put in a lightly oiled bowl. Rub a little oil over the surface of the dough to prevent it from drying out and cover loosely with plastic wrap or slide the bowl inside a clean plastic bag. Let rise in a warm place for 1 hour, or until doubled in size.

When the dough has increased to double its original size, turn out onto a lightly floured counter and punch down.

Shape the dough as required and place in a lightly greased baking pan or sheet. If placing in a pan, the dough should half-fill the pan.

Cover loosely again and let rise (prove) for a second time until doubled in size.

Bake in a hot oven. To test if the bread is cooked, turn out of the pan and tap the bottom. The loaf should sound hollow. Let cool on a wire rack.

Pizza dough

Makes 2 x 10-inch/25-cm pizzas

> $1^3/_4$ cups all-purpose flour, plus extra for dusting
>
> 1 tsp salt
>
> 6 tbsp lukewarm water
>
> 2 tbsp olive oil, plus extra for oiling
>
> 1 tsp active dry yeast

Sift the flour with the salt into a large, warmed bowl and make a well in the center. Add the water, oil, and yeast to the well. Using a wooden spoon or your hands, gradually mix, drawing the flour from the sides, to form a dough.

Turn out onto a lightly floured counter and knead for 5 minutes, or until smooth and elastic. Form the dough into a ball, put in a clean, lightly oiled bowl, and cover with oiled plastic wrap. Let rise in a warm place for 1 hour, or until doubled in size.

Turn out the dough onto a lightly floured counter and punch down. Knead briefly before shaping into 2 pizza bases.

Flaky pie pastry

scant 1⅝ cups all-purpose flour

8 tbsp unsalted butter

2–3 tbsp cold water

Sift the flour into a bowl. Cut the fat into small cubes and add to the flour. Rub in using your fingertips, lifting your hands high above the bowl to incorporate more air. The mixture will resemble fine breadcrumbs when the fat has been fully rubbed in.

Stir in any additional flavorings, if using, such as ground nuts, cheese, or sugar for sweet pastry.

Add the liquid all at once and use your fingers to bring the dough together. Turn out the dough onto a lightly floured counter and knead very lightly. Ideally, the dough should be wrapped in foil or plastic wrap and chilled in the refrigerator for 30 minutes to allow the dough to "relax," which helps to prevent it from shrinking when it is baked.

Roll out the dough on a lightly floured counter. Turn the dough as you roll. Use as required, then allow the dough to relax again in a cool place for 15–30 minutes before baking. This is especially important if you have not previously relaxed the dough.

Bake in a hot oven for 15–20 minutes until set. The temperature may then be reduced.

Flaky pie pastry can be made in a food processor, which helps keep it cooler than warm hands. Put the flour and fat in the processor and process until the mixture resembles fine breadcrumbs. The liquid can then be added to the machine, processing until the dough comes together.

Puff pastry

scant 2½ cups all-purpose flour

¾ cup unsalted butter

8 tbsp cold water

Sift the flour into a bowl and rub in one quarter of the butter.

Add the water and use your fingers to bring the dough together. Knead briefly to form a smooth dough. Put in a plastic bag and chill in the refrigerator for 30 minutes.

Roll out the remaining butter between two sheets of plastic wrap to form a block about ½ inch/1 cm thick.

Roll out the dough to a square about four times the size of the block of butter.

Put the block of butter in the center of the dough and fold over the corners of the dough to completely enclose the butter.

Roll out the dough into a rectangle 3 times as long as it is wide.

Fold one third of the dough over to cover the middle third, then fold the remainder over the top.

Give the dough a half turn, roll out to form another rectangle and fold again as before. Repeat the initial rolling and folding 6 times in total, chilling the dough frequently between rolling.

Let relax for a final 30 minutes, then use as required. Trim the folded edges of the dough before using to assist the rising. Bake in a hot oven. The pastry should rise to about 6 to 8 times its original height.

Chapter Content

Soups

Tomato soup

Serves 4

¼ cup butter

1 small onion, finely chopped

1 lb/450 g tomatoes, coarsely chopped

1 bay leaf

3 tbsp all-purpose flour

2½ cups milk

salt and pepper

sprigs of fresh basil, to garnish

Melt half the butter in a pan. Add the onion and cook over low heat, stirring occasionally, for 5–6 minutes until softened. Add the tomatoes and bay leaf and cook, stirring occasionally, for 15 minutes, or until pulpy.

Meanwhile, melt the remaining butter in another pan. Add the flour and cook, stirring continuously, for 1 minute. Remove the pan from the heat and gradually stir in the milk. Return to the heat, season with salt and pepper, and bring to a boil, stirring continuously. Continue to cook, stirring, until smooth and thickened.

When the tomatoes are pulpy, remove the pan from the heat. Discard the bay leaf and pour the tomato mixture into a food processor or blender. Process until smooth, then push through a fine strainer into a clean pan. Bring the tomato purée to a boil, then gradually stir it into the milk mixture. Season with salt and pepper to taste. Ladle into warmed bowls, garnish with basil, and serve immediately.

Chunky vegetable soup

Serves 6

2 carrots, sliced

1 onion, diced

1 garlic clove, crushed

12 oz/350 g new potatoes, diced

2 celery stalks, sliced

4 oz/115 g white mushrooms, quartered

14 oz/400 g canned chopped tomatoes

2½ cups Vegetable Stock (see page 20)

1 bay leaf

1 tsp dried mixed herbs or 1 tbsp chopped fresh mixed herbs

½ cup corn, frozen or canned, drained

½ cup shredded green cabbage

pepper

sprigs of fresh basil, to garnish (optional)

Put the carrots, onion, garlic, potatoes, celery, mushrooms, tomatoes, and stock into a large pan. Stir in the bay leaf and herbs. Bring to a boil, then reduce the heat, cover, and let simmer for 25 minutes.

Add the corn and cabbage and return to a boil. Reduce the heat, cover, and simmer for 5 minutes, or until the vegetables are tender. Remove and discard the bay leaf. Season with pepper to taste.

Ladle into warmed bowls, garnish with basil, if using, and serve immediately.

Chicken noodle soup

Serves 4–6

2 skinless chicken breasts

5 cups Chicken Stock (see page 21) or water

3 carrots, peeled and cut into ¼-inch/5-mm slices

3 oz/85 g vermicelli (or other small noodles)

salt and pepper

fresh tarragon leaves, to garnish

Place the chicken breasts in a large saucepan, add the stock, and bring to a simmer. Cook for 25–30 minutes. Skim any foam from the surface, if necessary. Remove the chicken from the stock and keep warm.

Continue to simmer the stock, add the carrots and vermicelli, and cook for 4–5 minutes.

Thinly slice or shred the chicken breasts and place in warmed serving dishes.

Season the soup with salt and pepper to taste and pour over the chicken. Serve immediately, garnished with the tarragon.

Creamy mushroom soup

Serves 4–6

3 tbsp butter

1 onion, chopped

1 lb 9 oz/700 g button mushrooms, coarsely chopped

3½ cups Vegetable Stock (see page 20)

3 tbsp chopped fresh tarragon, plus extra to garnish

⅔ cup sour cream

salt and pepper

Melt half the butter in a large pan. Add the onion and cook gently for 10 minutes, until softened. Add the remaining butter and the mushrooms and cook for 5 minutes, or until the mushrooms are browned.

Stir in the stock and tarragon, bring to a boil, then reduce the heat and simmer gently for 20 minutes. Transfer to a food processor or blender and process until smooth. Return the soup to the rinsed-out pan.

Stir in the sour cream and add salt and pepper to taste. Reheat the soup gently until hot. Ladle into warmed serving bowls and garnish with chopped tarragon. Serve at once.

French onion soup

Serves 6

1 lb 8 oz/675 g onions

3 tbsp olive oil

4 garlic cloves, 3 chopped and
1 peeled and halved

1 tsp sugar

2 tsp chopped fresh thyme, plus
extra sprigs to garnish

2 tbsp all-purpose flour

½ cup dry white wine

8½ cups Vegetable Stock
(see page 20)

6 slices French bread

10½ oz/300 g Gruyère cheese,
grated

Thinly slice the onions. Heat the oil in a large, heavy-bottom pan over medium–low heat, add the onions, and cook, stirring occasionally, for 10 minutes, or until they are just beginning to brown. Stir in the chopped garlic, sugar, and chopped thyme, then reduce the heat and cook, stirring occasionally, for 30 minutes, or until the onions are golden brown.

Sprinkle in the flour and cook, stirring continuously, for 1–2 minutes. Stir in the wine. Gradually stir in the stock and bring to a boil, skimming off any foam that rises to the surface, then reduce the heat and simmer for 45 minutes.

Meanwhile, preheat the broiler to medium. Toast the bread on both sides under the broiler, then rub the toast with the cut edges of the halved garlic clove.

Ladle the soup into 6 ovenproof bowls set on a baking sheet. Float a piece of toast in each bowl and divide the grated cheese among them. Place under the broiler for 2–3 minutes, or until the cheese has just melted. Garnish with thyme sprigs and serve immediately.

Minestrone

Serves 4

2 tbsp olive oil

2 garlic cloves, chopped

2 red onions, chopped

2¾ oz/75 g prosciutto, sliced

1 red bell pepper, seeded and
chopped

1 orange bell pepper, seeded and
chopped

14 oz/400 g canned chopped
tomatoes

4 cups Vegetable Stock
(see page 20)

1 celery stalk, trimmed and sliced

14 oz/400 g canned cranberry
beans, drained

1 cup shredded green leafy
cabbage

¾ cup frozen peas, thawed

1 tbsp chopped fresh parsley

2¾ oz/75 g dried vermicelli

salt and pepper

freshly grated Parmesan cheese,
to garnish

Heat the oil in a large pan. Add the garlic, onions, and prosciutto and cook over medium heat, stirring, for 3 minutes until slightly softened. Add the red and orange bell peppers and the chopped tomatoes and cook for an additional 2 minutes, stirring. Stir in the stock, then add the celery, cranberry beans, cabbage, peas, and parsley. Season with salt and pepper. Bring to a boil, then reduce the heat and simmer for 30 minutes.

Add the vermicelli to the pan. Cook for another 10–12 minutes, or according to the instructions on the package. Remove from the heat and ladle into serving bowls. Garnish with freshly grated Parmesan cheese and serve immediately.

My special recipes

....

....

....

....

....

....

....

....

....

....

....

....

....

Notes ....

....

....

....

....

My special recipes

....

....

....

....

....

....

....

....

....

....

....

....

....

....

Notes ....

....

....

....

....

My special recipes

....
....
....
....
....
....
....
....
....
....
....
....
....
....

Notes ....
....
....
....
....

My special recipes

....

....

....

....

....

....

....

....

....

....

....

....

....

....

....

Notes ....

....

....

....

....

My special recipes

....
....
....
....
....
....
....
....
....
....
....
....
....
....

Notes ....
....
....
....
....

My special recipes

....
....
....
....
....
....
....
....
....
....
....
....
....
....
....

Notes ....
....
....
....
....

Salads & vegetables

Salad greens & vegetables

Take a fresh look at salads and you'll see there are a lot of exciting developments in the salad bowl. Banished forever is the image of salads as dull dieters' food consisting of little more than limp lettuce and soggy, flavorless tomatoes.

Today, salads are one of the ultimate health foods. They can contain an exciting variety of colorful, delicious, and satisfying ingredients that provide the nutrients essential for healthy living. You'll find plenty of inspiration in this chapter for a cornucopia of healthy salads for all occasions, from light lunches and family meals to stylish dinner parties. Salads are versatile enough to cater for vegetarians and meat eaters alike. Meat, seafood, and poultry are ideal salad ingredients, along with the perhaps more commonly used lettuce and other leaves, vegetables, fruit, herbs, nuts, seeds, grains, legumes, and cheese. And with so many ingredients to choose from, salads can be as simple and light or complex and filling as you like. They also have the added bonus that they are versatile enough to fit easily into all your meal plans, from first courses through to desserts.

Inside this chapter you will find a selection of classic salads, including the all-time favorite Caesar Salad (see page 46). And if the idea of chicken salad no longer excites you because you have been making the same recipe for as long as you can remember, try a Waldorf Chicken Salad (see page 49). You'll never think of chicken salad as boring again!

Bowls of goodness

It wasn't long ago that when "salads" and "health" were linked it was in the context of weight-reducing diets that were restrictive and ultimately unsatisfying. Today, however, salads are a delicious component of a healthy diet, giving you endless variety at mealtimes without long hours in the kitchen.

With fresh produce from all corners of the globe readily available in supermarkets and gourmet food stores, you can enjoy a variety of salads all year round but, remember, salads are at their most flavorsome and nutritious when made with seasonal produce in its prime.

We are all being urged to eat more fruit and vegetables every day, and a salad a day can go a long way to help you meet the minimum target of 2½ cups for adults.

Served alongside a filling bowl of pasta or a plate of hot or cold roast meat, salads also make great accompaniments.

So, if you regularly fall back on the old favorite of just tossing a few green leaves with a simple oil-and-vinegar dressing, it's definitely time to think again. It's very easy to mix and match ingredients and the choice has never been greater. And don't make the mistake of thinking all salad ingredients have to be raw, either. Adding small amounts of cooked meat, poultry, and seafood to salad greens and other vegetables will give you a satisfying meal.

Cooked vegetables also make good salad ingredients. Broiled bell peppers, fried eggplants, blanched beans of all varieties, and peas are just some of the cooked vegetables you'll find will add flavor and an extra dimension to your salads.

Colorful greens

Even with so many ingredients to choose from, salad greens still provide the backbone of many popular salads. Take a look around your supermarket and you'll see leaves in many colors and textures, ranging from pearly, pale white Belgian endive to bright red and white radicchio. They also have a variety of flavors, from robust and peppery to sweet, nutty, and mild.

The greater the variety of leaves you include in your salad, the more interesting it will be, and the more nutrients it will contain. When you select salad greens, remember that the darker colored ones, such as spinach leaves, contain more beta-carotene, which help fight some forms of cancer and other illnesses. Leafy green vegetables are also excellent sources of fiber.

It's become very convenient to grab a bag of mixed salad greens at the supermarket, but it can be more satisfying to sample a selection of greens sold separately at farmers' markets. Asian and other ethnic food stores are also a good source of unusual greens.

Add a little variety
These new and familiar greens will add variety to your salad bowl:

• Arugula—known for their pronounced peppery flavor, these dark green leaves perk up many salads. They are popular in Italian salads. Substitute watercress if you can't find arugula.

• Beet greens—distinctive with their ruby-red stems, these soft leaves are mildly flavored.

• Mâche—also known as corn salad or lamb's lettuce, these tender leaves have a mild, slightly nutty flavor.

• Mesclun or mesclum—now sold in supermarkets, this French mix of leaves can include arugula, chervil, dandelion, and oak-leaf lettuce. Just add dressing and toss.

• Mizuna—from the Far East, this winter green has a full peppery flavor. Its pointy green leaves add visual interest to salads, too.

• Nasturtium—use both the colorful flowers and peppery leaves in salads.

• Radicchio—there is nothing like the bright red and white leaves of this member of the bitter endive family to enliven fall and early winter salads. It has a crisp texture and a deliciously nutty, peppery flavor.

• Red chard—like beet greens, these fiber-rich leaves have bright red stems and sometimes the leaves are tinged red as well.

• Romaine lettuce—Caesar Salad (see page 46) simply wouldn't be Caesar Salad without these long, crisp leaves. Romaine comes in a large, compact head with long, crisp leaves that have a sweet, nutty flavor.

Keep it fresh
Good salads are made with good ingredients, and freshness is all-important when buying salad greens. Because of the leaves' high water content, they are very perishable, so buy them as close as possible to serving. Not only will they taste better, they contain the most nutrients when in peak condition. Let your eyes guide you when shopping for salad greens—fresh leaves look fresh. They won't have any leaves tinged with brown, nor will they be wilted or slimy. When you get salad ingredients home, give them a rinse in cold water, then spin them dry or use a dish towel to pat them dry. Never let them soak in a sink of cold water because all the water-soluble vitamins and minerals will leach out. Use leafy ingredients as soon as possible, although most will keep for up to four days in a sealed container in the refrigerator. Once you open bags of prepared leaves, however, they should be used within 24 hours. You can prepare salad greens several hours in advance and store in the refrigerator, but do not dress until just before serving, because the acid in most dressings causes the leaves to wilt and become unappetizing.

Caesar salad

Serves 4

²⁄₃ cup olive oil

2 garlic cloves

5 slices white bread, crusts removed, cut into ²⁄₃-inch/1-cm cubes

1 large egg

2 romaine lettuces or 3 Boston lettuces

2 tbsp lemon juice

salt and pepper

8 canned anchovy fillets, drained and coarsely chopped

¾ cup fresh Parmesan cheese shavings

Bring a small, heavy-bottom pan of water to a boil.

Meanwhile, heat 4 tablespoons of the oil in a heavy-bottom skillet. Add the garlic and bread and cook, stirring and tossing frequently, for 4–5 minutes, or until the bread is crispy and golden all over. Remove from the skillet with a slotted spoon and drain on paper towels.

Add the egg to the boiling water and cook for 1 minute, then remove from the pan and set aside.

Arrange the salad greens in a salad bowl. Mix the remaining oil and the lemon juice together, then season with salt and pepper to taste. Crack the egg into the dressing and whisk to blend. Pour the dressing over the salad greens, toss well, then add the croûtons and chopped anchovies and toss the salad again. Sprinkle with Parmesan cheese shavings and serve.

Traditional Greek salad

Serves 4

7 oz/200 g feta cheese

½ head of iceberg lettuce or 1 lettuce such as romaine or escarole, shredded or sliced

4 tomatoes, quartered

½ cucumber, sliced

12 Greek black olives, pitted

2 tbsp chopped fresh herbs, such as oregano, flat-leaf parsley, mint, or basil

Dressing

6 tbsp extra virgin olive oil

2 tbsp fresh lemon juice

1 garlic clove, crushed

pinch of sugar

salt and pepper

Make the dressing by whisking together the oil, lemon juice, garlic, sugar, and salt and pepper to taste, in a small bowl. Set aside.

Cut the cheese into cubes about 1 inch/2.5 cm square. Put the lettuce, tomatoes, and cucumber in a salad bowl. Scatter over the cheese and toss together.

Just before serving, whisk the dressing, pour over the salad, and toss together. Scatter over the olives and chopped herbs and serve.

Salade Niçoise

Serves 4

2 tuna steaks, about ¾ inch/2 cm thick

olive oil, for brushing

salt and pepper

9 oz/250 g green beans, trimmed

½ cup vinaigrette or garlic vinaigrette dressing

2 hearts of lettuce, leaves separated

3 large hard-cooked eggs, quartered

2 juicy vine-ripened tomatoes, cut into wedges

1¾ oz/50 g anchovy fillets in oil, drained

2 oz/55 g Niçoise olives, pitted

Heat a grill pan over high heat until you can feel the heat rising from the surface. Brush the tuna steaks with oil, place them oiled side down on the hot pan, and cook for 2 minutes. Lightly brush the top side of the tuna steaks with more oil. Use a pair of tongs to turn over the steaks, then season with salt and pepper to taste. Continue cooking for an additional 2 minutes for rare or up to 4 minutes for well done. Let cool.

Meanwhile, bring a pan of lightly salted water to a boil. Add the beans to the pan and return to a boil, then boil for 3 minutes, or until just tender. Drain the beans and immediately transfer them to a large bowl. Pour over the vinaigrette and stir together, then let the beans cool in the dressing.

To serve, line a platter with lettuce leaves. Lift the beans out of the bowl, reserving the excess dressing, and pile them in the center of the platter. Break the tuna into large pieces and arrange it over the beans. Arrange the eggs and tomatoes around the side. Place the anchovy fillets over the salad, then scatter with the olives. Drizzle the remaining dressing over everything and serve.

Waldorf chicken salad

Serves 4

1 lb 2 oz red apples, cored and diced

3 tbsp fresh lemon juice

²/₃ cup light mayonnaise

1 head celery

4 shallots, sliced

1 garlic clove, finely chopped

³/₄ cup walnuts, chopped

1 lb 2 oz cooked chicken, cubed

1 romaine lettuce

pepper

chopped walnuts, to garnish

Place the apples in a bowl with the lemon juice and 1 tablespoon of the mayonnaise. Let stand for 40 minutes.

Using a sharp knife, slice the celery very thinly. Add the celery, shallots, garlic, and walnuts to the apple and mix. Stir in the mayonnaise and blend thoroughly.

Add the cooked chicken to the bowl and mix well.

Line a serving dish with the lettuce. Pile the chicken salad into a serving bowl, sprinkle with pepper, and garnish with the chopped walnuts.

Perfect roast potatoes

Serves 8

2½ oz/70 g goose or duck fat
or 5 tbsp olive oil

1 kg/2 lb 4 oz even-size potatoes,
peeled

coarse sea salt

8 fresh rosemary sprigs,
to garnish

Preheat the oven to 450°F/230°C. Put the fat in a large roasting pan, sprinkle generously with salt, and place in the oven.

Meanwhile, bring a large pan of lightly salted water to a boil, add the potatoes, and cook for 8–10 minutes until parboiled. Drain well and, if the potatoes are large, cut them in half. Return the potatoes to the empty pan and shake vigorously to roughen their outsides.

Arrange the potatoes in a single layer in the hot fat and roast for 45 minutes. If they look as if they are beginning to char around the edges, reduce the oven temperature to 400°F/200°C. Turn the potatoes over and roast for an additional 30 minutes until crisp. Serve garnished with rosemary sprigs.

Roasted vegetables

Serves 4

4 parsnips, scrubbed and trimmed but left unpeeled

4 carrots, scrubbed and trimmed but left unpeeled

2 white onions, quartered

1 red onion, quartered

3 leeks, trimmed and cut into 2½-inch/6-cm slices

6 garlic cloves, left unpeeled and whole

6 tbsp extra virgin olive oil

½ tsp mild chili powder

pinch of paprika

salt and pepper

Preheat the oven to 425°F/220°C. Bring a large pan of lightly salted water to a boil.

Cut the parsnips and carrots into wedges of similar size. Add them to the saucepan and cook for 5 minutes. Drain thoroughly and place in an ovenproof dish with the onions, leeks, and garlic. Pour over the oil, sprinkle with the spices and salt and pepper to taste, then mix until all the vegetables are well coated.

Roast in the preheated oven for at least 1 hour. Turn the vegetables from time to time until they are tender and starting to color. Remove from the oven, transfer to a warmed serving dish, and serve immediately.

My special recipes

....

....

....

....

....

....

....

....

....

....

....

....

....

Notes ....

....

....

....

....

My special recipes

....

....

....

....

....

....

....

....

....

....

....

....

....

....

....

Notes ....

....

....

....

....

My special recipes

....

....

....

....

....

....

....

....

....

....

....

....

....

....

Notes ....

....

....

....

....

My special recipes

....

....

....

....

....

....

....

....

....

....

....

....

....

....

Notes ....

....

....

....

....

....

My special recipes

....
....
....
....
....
....
....
....
....
....
....
....
....
....

Notes ....
....
....
....
....

My special recipes

....
....
....
....
....
....
....
....
....
....
....
....
....
....
....

Notes ....
....
....
....
....

Pasta & grains

Making fresh pasta

For convenience, most of the recipes in this book use dried pasta. However, if you want to try making filled pasta, such as ravioli, you will need to prepare the dough yourself. Making fresh pasta is not as difficult as you may believe and the same basic dough can also be used to make lasagna sheets and a variety of shapes, such as tagliatelle, pappardelle, and macaroni. You won't need any special equipment (a pasta machine makes the job of rolling the dough simpler but it's not strictly necessary) and the process is both easy and satisfying.

Basic pasta dough

Serves 3–4

$1^3/_4$ cups white bread flour, plus extra for dusting

pinch of salt

2 eggs, lightly beaten

1 tbsp olive oil

Sift the flour and salt together onto a counter and make a well in the center with your fingers. Pour the eggs and oil into the well, then, using the fingers of one hand, gradually incorporate the flour into the liquid. Knead the dough on a lightly floured counter until it is completely smooth. Wrap in plastic wrap and let rest for 30 minutes before rolling out or feeding through a pasta machine. Resting makes the dough more elastic.

Flavored pasta

Basic pasta dough may be flavored and colored by the addition of different ingredients.

Tomato pasta: Add 2 tablespoons of tomato paste to the well in the flour and use only $1^1/_2$ eggs instead of 2.

Spinach pasta: Blanch 8 oz/225 g spinach in boiling water for 1 minute, then drain, and squeeze out as much liquid as possible. Alternatively, use $5^1/_2$ oz/150 g thawed frozen spinach. This does not need blanching, but as much liquid as possible should be squeezed out. Finely chop the spinach and mix with the flour before making a well and adding the eggs and oil.

Herb pasta: Add 3 tablespoons of finely chopped fresh herbs to the flour before making a well and adding the eggs and oil.

Whole wheat pasta: Use $1^1/_4$ cups whole wheat flour with $^1/_4$ cup white bread flour.

Rolling out pasta dough

When the fresh dough has rested, it may be rolled out by hand or with a pasta machine. Large quantities of dough should be halved or cut into thirds before rolling out. Keep covered until you are ready to work on them. To roll out by hand, lightly dust a counter with all-purpose flour, then roll out the pasta dough with a lightly floured rolling pin, always rolling away from you and turning the dough a quarter turn each time. Keep rolling

to make a rectangle $^1/_{16}$–$^1/_8$ inch/ 2–3 mm thick. The dough can then be cut into ribbons, stamped out with a cookie cutter, or filled and cut out to make ravioli.

A pasta machine makes rolling out the dough easier and quicker and ensures that it is even. There are a number of models available, the most useful being a hand-cranked machine with attachable cutters. An electric machine is even easier to use but somewhat extravagant. Cut the dough into manageable-size pieces— 1 quantity Basic Pasta Dough should be cut into 4 pieces, for example. Flatten a piece with your hand and wrap the others in plastic wrap until required. Fold the flat piece into thirds and feed it through the pasta machine on its widest setting. Repeat the folding and rolling 3 or 4 more times on this setting, then close the rollers by one notch. Continue feeding the dough through the rollers, without folding into thirds, gradually reducing the setting until you reach the narrowest. If you want to make ribbons, cut the dough into 12-inch/30-cm strips and feed through the appropriate cutter.

Pasta sauces

Tomato Sauce

Serves 4

2 tbsp olive oil

1 small onion, chopped

1 garlic clove, finely chopped

14 oz/400 g canned chopped tomatoes

2 tbsp chopped fresh flat-leaf parsley

1 tsp dried oregano

2 bay leaves

2 tbsp tomato paste

1 tsp sugar

salt and pepper

Heat the oil in a pan. Add the onion and garlic and cook over low heat, stirring occasionally, for 5 minutes until softened.

Increase the heat to medium, stir in the tomatoes, parsley, oregano, bay leaves, tomato paste, and sugar, and season with salt and pepper to taste.

Bring to a boil, then reduce the heat and simmer, uncovered, for 15–20 minutes until reduced by half. Taste and adjust the seasoning, if necessary. Remove and discard the bay leaves.

Italian Cheese Sauce

Serves 4–6

4 tbsp butter

2 tbsp all-purpose flour

$1^1/_4$ cups hot milk

pinch of ground nutmeg

pinch of dried thyme

2 tbsp white wine vinegar

3 tbsp heavy cream

$^1/_2$ cup grated mozzarella cheese

$^1/_2$ cup grated Parmesan cheese

1 tsp English mustard

2 tbsp sour cream

salt and pepper

Melt the butter in a pan and stir in the flour. Cook, stirring, over low heat until the mixture is light in color and crumbly in texture. Stir in the hot milk and cook, stirring, for 15 minutes until thick and smooth.

Add the nutmeg, thyme, and vinegar and season to taste. Stir in the cream and mix well.

Stir in the cheeses, mustard, and sour cream and mix until the cheeses have melted and blended into the sauce.

Pesto

Serves 4

2 handfuls fresh basil leaves

$^1/_4$ cup pine nuts

1 garlic clove, coarsely chopped

$^1/_2$ cup freshly grated Parmesan cheese

6–8 tbsp extra virgin olive oil

salt

Put the basil, pine nuts, and garlic in a mortar. Add a pinch of salt and pound to a paste with a pestle.

Transfer the mixture to a bowl and gradually work in the cheese with a wooden spoon.

Gradually stir in the oil until the sauce is thick and creamy. Cover with plastic wrap and store in the refrigerator until ready to use.

Spaghetti bolognese

Serves 4

1 tbsp olive oil

1 onion, finely chopped

2 garlic cloves, chopped

1 carrot, chopped

1 celery stalk, chopped

1¾ oz/50 g pancetta or bacon, diced

¾ cup lean ground beef

14 oz/400 g canned chopped tomatoes

2 tsp dried oregano

½ cup red wine

2 tbsp tomato paste

12 oz/350 g dried spaghetti

salt and pepper

chopped fresh flat-leaf parsley, to garnish

Heat the oil in a large skillet. Add the onion and cook for 3 minutes. Add the garlic, carrot, celery, and pancetta and sauté for 3–4 minutes, or until they are just beginning to brown.

Add the beef and cook over high heat for another 3 minutes, or until all of the meat is browned. Stir in the tomatoes, oregano, and red wine and bring to a boil. Reduce the heat and simmer for about 45 minutes.

Stir in the tomato paste and season with salt and pepper.

Bring a large pan of lightly salted water to a boil, add the spaghetti, and cook for 8–10 minutes, or until tender but still firm to the bite. Drain thoroughly.

Transfer the spaghetti to a serving plate and pour over the sauce. Toss to mix well, garnish with parsley, and serve hot.

Tagliatelle alla carbonara

Serves 4

1 lb/450 g dried tagliatelle

1 tbsp olive oil

8 oz/225 g rindless pancetta or
lean bacon, chopped

4 eggs

5 tbsp light cream

2 tbsp freshly grated Parmesan
cheese

salt and pepper

Bring a large, heavy-bottom pan of lightly salted water to a boil. Add the pasta,
return to a boil, and cook for 8–10 minutes, or until tender but still firm to the bite.

Meanwhile, heat the oil in a heavy-bottom skillet. Add the pancetta and cook over
medium heat, stirring frequently, for 8–10 minutes.

Beat the eggs with the cream in a small bowl and season to taste with salt and
pepper. Drain the pasta and return it to the pan. Add the contents of the skillet,
then add the egg mixture and half the Parmesan cheese. Stir well, then transfer to
a warmed serving dish. Serve immediately, sprinkled with the remaining cheese.

Spinach & ricotta ravioli

Serves 4

12 oz/350 g fresh spinach leaves,
coarse stalks removed

1 cup ricotta cheese

½ cup freshly grated Parmesan
cheese, plus extra to serve

2 eggs

pinch of freshly grated nutmeg

1 quantity Spinach Pasta Dough
(see page 60)

all-purpose flour, for dusting

salt and pepper

To make the filling, place the spinach in a heavy-bottom pan with just the water clinging to the leaves after washing, then cover and cook over low heat for 5 minutes, or until wilted. Drain well and squeeze out as much moisture as possible. Let cool, then chop finely.

Beat the ricotta until smooth, then stir in the spinach, Parmesan cheese, and 1 egg, and season with nutmeg and pepper.

Divide the pasta in half and wrap 1 piece in plastic wrap. Roll out the other piece on a lightly floured counter to a rectangle ¹/₁₆–¹/₈ inch/2–3 mm thick. Cover with a damp dish towel and roll out the other piece of dough to the same size. Place teaspoonfuls of the filling in rows 1¹/₂ inches/4 cm apart on a sheet of pasta dough. In a small bowl, lightly beat the remaining egg and use it to brush the spaces between the mounds. Lift the second sheet of dough on top of the first and press down firmly between the pockets of filling, pushing out any air bubbles. Using a pasta wheel or sharp knife, cut into squares. Place on a floured dish towel and let stand for 1 hour.

Bring a large, heavy-bottom pan of lightly salted water to a boil, add the ravioli, in batches, return to a boil, and cook for 5 minutes. Remove with a slotted spoon and drain on paper towels. Transfer to a warmed serving dish and serve immediately, sprinkled with Parmesan cheese.

Beef lasagne with ricotta cheese

Serves 6

¾ cup olive oil

4 tbsp butter

½ cup diced bacon or pancetta

1 onion, finely chopped

1 celery stalk, finely chopped

1 carrot, finely chopped

12 oz/350 g beef pot roast, in a single piece

5 tbsp red wine

2 tbsp sun-dried tomato paste

7 oz/200 g Italian sausage

2 eggs

1⅓ cups freshly grated Parmesan cheese

½ cup fresh breadcrumbs

1½ cups ricotta cheese

8 dried no-precook lasagne sheets

12 oz/350 g mozzarella cheese, sliced

salt and pepper

chopped fresh parsley, to garnish

Heat ½ cup of the oil with the butter in a large pan. Add the bacon, onion, celery, and carrot and cook over low heat, until softened. Increase the heat to medium, add the beef, and cook until evenly browned.

Stir in the wine and tomato paste, season with salt and pepper, and bring to a boil. Reduce the heat, cover, and simmer gently, for 1½ hours until the beef is tender.

Meanwhile, heat 2 tablespoons of the remaining oil in a skillet. Add the sausage and cook for 8–10 minutes. Remove from the skillet and discard the skin. Thinly slice the sausage and set aside.

Transfer the beef to a cutting board and dice finely. Return half the beef to the sauce. Mix the remaining beef in a bowl with 1 egg, 1 tablespoon of the Parmesan cheese, and the breadcrumbs. Shape into walnut-size balls. Heat the remaining oil in a skillet, add the meatballs, and cook for 5–8 minutes, until browned.

Pass the ricotta cheese through a strainer into a bowl. Stir in the remaining egg and 4 tablespoons of the remaining Parmesan cheese.

Preheat the oven to 350°F/180°C. In a rectangular ovenproof dish, make layers with the lasagne sheets, ricotta mixture, meat sauce, meatballs, sausage, and mozzarella. Finish with a layer of the ricotta cheese mixture and sprinkle with the remaining Parmesan cheese.

Bake the lasagne in the preheated oven for 20–25 minutes, until cooked through and bubbling. Serve, garnished with parsley.

Chili con carne

Serves 4

1 lb 10 oz/750 g lean braising beef

2 tbsp vegetable oil

1 large onion, sliced

2–4 garlic cloves, crushed

1 tbsp all-purpose flour

generous 1¾ cups tomato juice

14 oz/400 g canned tomatoes

1–2 tbsp sweet chili sauce

1 tsp ground cumin

salt and pepper

15 oz/425 g canned red kidney
beans, drained and rinsed

½ tsp dried oregano

1–2 tbsp chopped fresh parsley

sprigs of fresh herbs, to garnish

freshly cooked rice and tortillas,
to serve

Preheat the oven to 325°F/160°C. Using a sharp knife, cut the beef into

¾-inch/2-cm cubes. Heat the vegetable oil in a large flameproof casserole and

cook the beef over medium heat until well sealed on all sides. Remove the beef

from the casserole with a slotted spoon and set aside until required.

Add the onion and garlic to the casserole and cook until lightly browned, then stir

in the flour and cook for 1–2 minutes.

Stir in the tomato juice and tomatoes and bring to a boil. Return the beef to the

casserole and add the chili sauce, cumin, and salt and pepper to taste. Cover and

cook in the preheated oven for 1½ hours, or until the beef is almost tender.

Stir in the kidney beans, oregano, and parsley, and adjust the seasoning to taste,

if necessary. Cover the casserole and return to the oven for 45 minutes. Transfer

to 4 large, warmed serving plates, garnish with sprigs of fresh herbs, and serve

immediately with freshly cooked rice and tortillas.

Parmesan cheese risotto with mushrooms

serves 4

4 cups Vegetable Stock (see page 20) or Chicken Stock (see page 21)

2 tbsp olive oil or vegetable oil

generous 1 cup risotto rice

2 garlic cloves, crushed

1 onion, chopped

2 celery stalks, chopped

1 red or green bell pepper, seeded and chopped

8 oz/225 g mushrooms, thinly sliced

1 tbsp chopped fresh oregano or 1 tsp dried oregano

¼ cup sun-dried tomatoes in olive oil, drained and chopped (optional)

½ cup finely grated Parmesan cheese

salt and pepper

fresh flat-leaf parsley sprigs or bay leaves, to garnish

Bring the stock to a boil in a pan, then reduce the heat and keep simmering gently over low heat while you are cooking the risotto.

Heat the oil in a deep pan. Add the rice and cook over low heat, stirring continuously, for 2–3 minutes, until the grains are thoroughly coated in oil and translucent.

Add the garlic, onion, celery, and bell pepper and cook, stirring frequently, for 5 minutes. Add the mushrooms and cook for 3–4 minutes. Stir in the oregano.

Gradually add the hot stock, a ladleful at a time. Stir continuously and add more liquid as the rice absorbs each addition. Increase the heat to medium so that the liquid bubbles. Cook for 20 minutes, or until all the liquid is absorbed and the rice is creamy. Add the sun-dried tomatoes, if using, 5 minutes before the end of the cooking time and season with salt and pepper to taste.

Remove the risotto from the heat and stir in half the Parmesan cheese until it melts. Transfer the risotto to warmed plates. Top with the remaining cheese, garnish with flat-leaf parsley or bay leaves, and serve at once.

My special recipes

....

....

....

....

....

....

....

....

....

....

....

....

....

....

Notes ....

....

....

....

....

My special recipes

....

....

....

....

....

....

....

....

....

....

....

....

....

....

Notes ....

....

....

....

....

My special recipes

....

....

....

....

....

....

....

....

....

....

....

....

....

Notes ....

....

....

....

....

My special recipes

....

....

....

....

....

....

....

....

....

....

....

....

....

....

Notes ....

....

....

....

....

My special recipes

....

....

....

....

....

....

....

....

....

....

....

....

....

Notes ....

....

....

....

....

....

My special recipes

....

....

....

....

....

....

....

....

....

....

....

....

....

....

Notes ....

....

....

....

....

Chapter Content

Meat

Choosing meat

Terms applied to different varieties of a particular meat, such as lamb, are often related to the age of the animal. The meat of younger animals is generally more tender, but also less pronounced in flavor, while the meat of older animals is likely to be tougher yet tastier.

Beef and veal

Beef is the meat provided by domestic cattle, while veal is the meat of the young calf. Beef comes from cattle slaughtered at over 1 year old, and veal from male calves slaughtered at 1–3 months old. Baby beef refers to the lean and tender meat from a calf of 7–10 months old. It is not as flavorful as meat from older cattle.

The USDA standard grades of beef available to the consumer, starting with the highest quality grade, are prime, choice, select, standard, and commercial.

Lamb and mutton

Lamb is the meat from a young sheep, and there are several types.
Baby lamb: milk-fed lamb slaughtered at 6–8 weeks old.
Spring lamb: from 3–5 months old and weighing 20–40 lb/9.1–18 kg.
Regular lamb: 5–12 months, and most commonly available.
Yearling: meat from a lamb that is 1–2 years old.
Mutton: meat of a mature sheep over 2 years old.

Pork, ham, and bacon

Pork is the fresh meat of the domesticated pig. Traditionally, pork was seasonal meat, much of which was salted and preserved to provide ham, bacon, and sausages. Most pork is slaughtered at 6–9 months.

Meat specialties

There are other edible parts of an animal left when the meat is removed from the carcass. This includes organs such as heart, liver, and kidneys, as well as tongue, brain, thymus gland (sweetbreads), stomach lining (tripe), and blood (used in blood pudding). Pig's feet/trotters, head, and cheek, ox tail, and calf's foot fall into this category, too.

Cooking times & temperatures

Thorough cooking of meat is very important, particularly in the case of pork, which can carry harmful bacteria and cause food poisoning if not cooked all the way through. It's essential to set the oven to the correct temperature and cook for the time recommended for the weight of the piece of meat. A meat thermometer is a useful device for testing whether a joint of meat is cooked thoroughly. Simply insert the thermometer into the thickest part of the meat at the start of cooking, being careful to avoid contact with any bone, which might produce a false reading. When the thermometer reaches the required temperature, the meat is cooked.

Beef

Preheat the oven to 450°F/230°C. Roast for 20 minutes, then reduce the temperature to 375°F/190°C and roast for:

- 15 minutes per 1 lb/450 g for rare
- 20 minutes per 1 lb/450 g for medium
- 30 minutes per 1 lb/450 g for well done.

Meat thermometer recommended internal temperature:
Rare: 140°F/60°C
Medium: 160°F/71°C
Well done: 169°F/76°C.

Lamb

Preheat the oven to 375°F/190°C.

Roast for 30 minutes per 1 lb/ 450 g, 30 minutes less for rare.

Meat thermometer recommended internal temperature: 180°F/82°C.

Pork

Preheat the oven to 450°F/230°C:

Roast for 25 minutes, then reduce the temperature to 375°F/190°C and roast for 35 minutes per 1 lb/450 g.

Meat thermometer recommended internal temperature:
Pork: 189°F/87°C
Bacon/gammon joint: 160°F/71°C.

Roast beef

Serves 8

1 beef rib roast, weighing 6 lb/2.7 kg

2 tsp English dry mustard

1 tbsp all-purpose flour

red wine (optional)

salt and pepper

Beef Gravy and Quick Horseradish Sauce (see page 79), to serve

Preheat the oven to 450°F/230°C. Season the meat with salt and pepper to taste and rub in the mustard and the flour.

Put the meat in a roasting pan large enough to hold it comfortably and roast in the preheated oven for 15 minutes. Reduce the heat to 375°F/190°C and cook for 1 hour 45 minutes for rare beef or 2 hours 20 minutes for medium beef. Baste the meat occasionally to keep it moist. If the pan becomes too dry, add a little red wine.

When the meat is cooked, transfer to a warmed serving plate, cover loosely with foil, and let rest for 10–15 minutes.

When ready to serve, carve the meat into slices and serve on warmed plates. Serve with the Beef Gravy in a warmed pitcher, and with some Quick Horseradish Sauce on the side.

Quick horseradish sauce

Serves 8

6 tbsp creamed horseradish sauce

6 tbsp sour cream

Mix the horseradish sauce and sour cream together in a small bowl until well blended. Serve the sauce with roast beef.

Beef gravy

Serves 8

pan juices from a meat roasting pan

2 tbsp flour

1¼ cups red wine

1¼ cups Beef Stock (see page 21)

Worcestershire sauce (optional)

salt and pepper

Pour off most of the fat from the roasting pan, leaving behind the meat juices and the sediment. Put the roasting pan over medium heat and scrape all the sediment from the bottom of the pan. Sprinkle in the flour and quickly mix it into the juices with a small whisk. When you have a smooth paste, gradually add the wine and most of the stock, whisking continuously. Bring to a boil, then reduce the heat to a gentle simmer and cook for 2–3 minutes. Season with salt and pepper to taste and add the remaining stock, if necessary, and a little Worcestershire sauce, if using.

Roast pork

Serves 4

1 boned pork loin joint, weighing
2 lb 4 oz/1 kg, rind removed and
reserved

2 tbsp mustard

salt and pepper

Apple sauce

1 lb/450 g cooking apples, peeled,
cored and sliced

3 tablespoons water

1 tbsp superfine sugar

pinch of ground cinnamon
(optional)

1 tbsp butter (optional)

Gravy

1 tbsp flour

1¼ cups hard cider, apple juice, or
Chicken Stock
(see page 21)

salt and pepper

Preheat the oven to 400°F/200°C. Score the pork rind with a sharp knife and sprinkle with salt. Put it on a wire rack set over a baking tray and roast in the preheated oven for 30–40 minutes until the crackling is golden and crisp.

Season the pork well with salt and pepper and spread the fat with the mustard. Put in a roasting pan and roast in the center of the oven for 20 minutes. Reduce the temperature to 375°F/190°C and cook for an additional 50–60 minutes until the meat is well browned and the juices run clear when a skewer is inserted into the thickest part of the meat. Remove the meat from the oven and transfer to a warmed serving plate, cover loosely with foil, and let rest in a warm place.

Meanwhile, to make the sauce, put all the ingredients into a pan over low heat. Cook for 10 minutes, stirring occasionally. Beat well until the sauce is thick and smooth—use an electric mixer for a smooth finish.

To make the gravy, pour off most of the fat from the roasting pan. Place the pan over medium heat and scrape the sediment from the bottom. Sprinkle in the flour and quickly whisk it into the juices. When you have a smooth paste, gradually add the cider, whisking continuously. Bring to a boil, reduce the heat, and simmer for 2–3 minutes until thick. Season with salt and pepper, pour into a warmed serving pitcher, and serve with the pork, with some Apple Sauce on the side.

Roast lamb

Serves 6

1 leg of lamb, weighing
3 lb 5 oz/1.5 kg

6 garlic cloves, thinly sliced
lengthwise

8 fresh rosemary sprigs

4 tbsp olive oil

salt and pepper

Red currant glaze

4 tbsp red currant jelly

1¼ cups rosé wine

Preheat the oven to 400°F/200°C. Using a small, sharp knife, cut slits all over the leg of lamb. Insert 1–2 garlic slices and 4–5 rosemary needles into each slit. Put any remaining rosemary in the bottom of a roasting pan. Season the lamb with salt and pepper to taste and put in the roasting pan. Pour over the oil. Cover with foil and roast in the preheated oven for 1 hour 20 minutes.

To make the glaze, mix the red currant jelly and wine together in a small pan. Heat over low heat, stirring continuously, until combined. Bring to a boil, then reduce the heat and simmer until the glaze is reduced. Remove the lamb from the oven and pour over the glaze. Return to the oven and roast, uncovered, for about 10 minutes, depending on how well done you like it.

Remove the lamb from the roasting pan and transfer to a cutting board. Cover loosely with foil and let rest for 15 minutes before carving and serving.

The classic hamburger

Serves 4–6

1 lb/450 g sirloin or top round, freshly ground

1 onion, grated

2–4 garlic cloves, crushed

2 tsp whole grain mustard

pepper

2 tbsp olive oil

1 lb/450 g onions, finely sliced

2 tsp brown sugar

hamburger buns, to serve

Place the ground beef, onion, garlic, mustard, and pepper in a large bowl and mix together. Shape into 4–6 equal-size burgers, then cover and let chill for 30 minutes.

Meanwhile, heat the oil in a heavy-bottom skillet. Add the onions and sauté over low heat for 10–15 minutes, or until the onions have caramelized. Add the sugar after 8 minutes and stir occasionally during cooking. Drain well on paper towels and keep warm.

Preheat the grill. Cook the burgers over hot coals for 3–5 minutes on each side or until cooked to personal preference. Serve in hamburger buns with the onions.

Peppered T-bone steak

Serves 2

2 tbsp whole black peppercorns, green peppercorns, or a mixture of both

2 T-bone steaks, about 9 oz/250 g each

2 tbsp butter

1 tbsp olive or sunflower oil

$\frac{1}{2}$ cup red wine

salt

freshly cooked vegetables, to serve

Put the peppercorns into a mortar and coarsely crush with a pestle, or put into a strong plastic bag, place on a cutting board, and coarsely crush with the end of a rolling pin.

Spread out the crushed peppercorns on a plate and press one side of each steak hard into them to encrust the surface of the meat. Turn over and repeat with the other side.

Melt the butter with the oil in a large, heavy-bottom skillet over high heat. When hot, add the steaks, and cook quickly on both sides to seal. Reduce the heat to medium and cook, turning once, for $2\frac{1}{2}$–3 minutes each side for rare, $3\frac{1}{2}$–5 minutes each side for medium, or 5–7 minutes each side for well done. Transfer the steaks to warmed plates and keep warm.

Add the wine to the skillet and stir to deglaze by scraping any sediment from the bottom of the skillet. Bring to a boil and boil until reduced by about half. Season to taste with salt. Pour the pan juices over the steaks and serve at once with freshly cooked vegetables.

My special recipes

....

....

....

....

....

....

....

....

....

....

....

....

....

....

Notes ....

....

....

....

....

My special recipes

....

....

....

....

....

....

....

....

....

....

....

....

....

....

Notes ....

....

....

....

....

My special recipes

....

....

....

....

....

....

....

....

....

....

....

....

....

Notes ....

....

....

....

....

My special recipes

....

....

....

....

....

....

....

....

....

....

....

....

....

....

Notes ....

....

....

....

....

My special recipes

....

....

....

....

....

....

....

....

....

....

....

....

....

Notes ....

....

....

....

....

My special recipes

....
....
....
....
....
....
....
....
....
....
....
....
....
....
....

Notes ....
....
....
....
....

Poultry

Choosing poultry

Poultry is defined as domestic fowl bred specifically for eating. Raised for their meat and eggs, poultry includes chicken, turkey, duck, and goose.

Chicken

Chicken is the most popular and widely available form of poultry. It is sold under a number of different names according to its age, size, and method of rearing. The following are the most common types of chicken:

Poussin: an immature chicken, 4–6 weeks old, weighing up to 1 lb/450 g, with delicate, moist meat.

Broiler-fryer: the most common bird for broiling or frying. A bird can weigh up to 3½ lb/1.6 kg and is generally about 10 weeks old.

Stewing chicken: an older bird, usually a laying hen weighing 6 lb/2.7 kg.

Capon: a castrated young chicken bred for its tender, white flesh.

Cornish hen: this hybrid chicken is also referred to as a Rock Cornish hen. It is a small bird, weighing up to 2½ lb/1 kg.

Free-range: indicates that a limited number of birds are housed per square yard/meter and have outside access for at least half their life. They weigh an average of 4½ lb/2 kg and are slaughtered at 10–12 weeks.

Battery: intensively reared chickens with no outside access, slaughtered at 6 weeks.

Organic: chickens raised according to a strictly regulated standard of welfare. They are GM-free and have been fed with antibiotic-free food, with guaranteed access to forage and feed outside.

Turkey

Descended from the North American wild turkey, this domesticated bird is available all year round. A young turkey weighing 8–24 lb/3.6–11 kg will provide about 70 percent white meat and 30 percent dark meat. Allow an average of 12 oz/ 350 g per person. The rearing methods for turkeys are similar to chickens, so an organic, free-range bird will have a better flavor and texture than an intensively raised bird.

Duck

Duck is a waterfowl, now mainly raised commercially and widely available. There are a number of varieties, and as with all poultry, a younger, free-range bird will taste better than an older, farmed bird. Most duck on offer is duckling, which is 6–8 weeks old, but duck up to 16 weeks old is sometimes sold. A 6-lb/2.7-kg duck will feed 2–3 people.

Goose

Goose is a large water bird popular for roasting and raised free range. Fatty and with rich, dark meat, it has an average weight of 6–12 lb/ 2.7–5.4 kg, but because of its meat to fat ratio, a goose will feed only four people, on average.

Cooking times & temperatures

It is essential to cook poultry all the way through in order to kill off any potentially harmful bacteria. It is important to remember that individual oven temperatures and cooking times vary, so the recommended cooking times are only approximate. You can check whether a bird is cooked by inserting a sharp knife or skewer into the thickest part; if the juices run clear, it is cooked. If not, return it to the oven and cook until done. Alternatively, you can insert a meat thermometer into the thickest part of the bird at the start of cooking, avoiding contact with any bone, which may produce a false reading. The bird is cooked when the temperature reaches 194°F/90°C.

Chicken
Preheat the oven to 375°F/190°C.

Roast for 20 minutes per 1 lb/ 450 g, plus 20 minutes. Increase the temperature to 425°F/220°C for the final 15 minutes of the calculated time.

Turkey
Preheat the oven to 425°F/220°C.

For turkeys weighing 8–10 lb/ 3.5–4.5 kg, roast for 30 minutes, then reduce the temperature to 325°F/160°C for 2½–3 hours, increasing the temperature to 400°F/200°C, uncovered, for the final 30 minutes.

For turkeys weighing 12–14 lb/ 5.5–6.5 kg, roast, uncovered, for 40 minutes, then reduce the temperature to 325°F/160°C for 3–3½ hours, increasing the temperature to 400°F/200°C for the final 30 minutes.

Duck
Preheat the oven to 425°F/220°C.

Roast for 20 minutes, then reduce the temperature to 350°F/180°C and roast for 1 hour–1 hour 10 minutes.

Goose
Preheat the oven to 425°F/220°C.

Roast for 20 minutes, then reduce the temperature to 350°F/180°C and roast for 1 hour 20 minutes–2 hours.

Traditional roast chicken

Serves 6

1 x 5-lb/2.25-kg free-range chicken

2 tbsp butter

2 tbsp chopped fresh lemon thyme

1 lemon, quartered

½ cup white wine

salt and pepper

6 fresh thyme sprigs, to garnish

Preheat the oven to 425°F/220°C. Make sure the chicken is clean, wiping it inside and out with paper towels, and place in a roasting pan. In a bowl, soften the butter with a fork, mix in the thyme, and season well with salt and pepper. Butter the chicken all over with the herb butter, inside and out, and place the lemon pieces inside the body cavity. Pour the wine over the chicken.

Roast in the center of the preheated oven for 20 minutes. Reduce the temperature to 375°F/190°C and roast for an additional 1¼ hours, basting frequently. Cover with foil if the skin begins to brown too much. If the pan dries out, add a little more wine or water.

Test that the chicken is cooked by piercing the thickest part of the leg with a sharp knife or skewer and making sure the juices run clear. Remove from the oven. Transfer the chicken to a warmed serving plate, cover loosely with foil, and let rest for 10 minutes before carving. Place the roasting pan on the stove and bubble the juices gently over low heat until they have reduced and are thick and glossy. Season with salt and pepper to taste. Serve the chicken with the juices and scatter with the thyme sprigs.

Boned & stuffed roast duck

Serves 6–8

4 lb duck/1.8 kg (dressed weight); ask your butcher to bone the duck and cut off the wings at the first joint

450 g/1 lb flavored sausage meat, such as pork and apricot

1 small onion, finely chopped

1 apple, cored and finely chopped

3 oz/85 g dried apricots, finely chopped

¾ cup chopped walnuts

2 tbsp chopped fresh parsley

1 large or 2 smaller duck breasts, skin removed

salt and pepper

Apricot sauce

400 g/14 oz canned apricot halves, in syrup

⅔ cup Chicken Stock (see page 21)

½ cup Marsala

½ tbsp ground cinnamon

½ tbsp ground ginger

salt and pepper

Preheat the oven to 375°F/190°C. Wipe the duck with paper towels both inside and out. Lay it, skin side down, on a board and season well with salt and pepper.

Mix together the sausage meat, onion, apple, apricots, walnuts, and parsley and season well with salt and pepper. Form into a large sausage shape.

Lay the duck breast(s) on the whole duck and cover with the stuffing. Wrap the whole duck around the filling and tuck in any leg and neck flaps. Sew the duck up the back and across both ends with fine string. Try to use one piece of string so that you can remove it all at once. Mold the duck into a good shape and place, sewn side down, on a wire rack over a roasting pan. Roast for 1½–2 hours, basting occasionally. When it is cooked, the duck should be golden brown and crispy.

Meanwhile, make the sauce. Whiz the apricot halves with their syrup in a blender until a purée forms. Pour the purée into a pan and add the stock, Marsala, cinnamon, and ginger and season with salt and pepper to taste. Stir over low heat, then simmer for 2–3 minutes.

Carve the duck into thick slices at the table and serve with the warm apricot sauce.

Roast turkey

Serves 8

1 quantity ready-prepared stuffing

1 x 11-lb/5-kg turkey

1½ tbsp butter

Bread Sauce (see page 97) and
Cranberry Sauce (see page 97),
to serve

Preheat the oven to 425°F/220°C. Spoon the stuffing into the neck cavity of the

turkey and close the flap of skin with a skewer. Place the bird in a large roasting

pan and rub it all over with the butter. Roast in the preheated oven for 1 hour, then

reduce the oven temperature to 350°F/180°C and roast for an additional 2½ hours.

You may need to pour off the fat from the roasting pan occasionally.

Check that the turkey is cooked by inserting a skewer or the point of a sharp knife

into the thigh—if the juices run clear, it is ready. Transfer the bird to a cutting

board, cover loosely with foil, and let rest.

Carve the turkey and serve with the warm Bread Sauce and the Cranberry Sauce.

Bread sauce

Serves 8

1 onion, peeled

4 cloves

2½ cups milk

2 cups fresh white
breadcrumbs

2 tbsp butter

salt and pepper

Stud the onion with the cloves, then place in a pan with the milk, breadcrumbs, and butter. Bring just to boiling point over low heat, then remove from the heat and let stand in a warm place to infuse. Just before serving, remove the onion and cloves and reheat the sauce gently, beating well with a wooden spoon. Season with salt and pepper to taste.

Cranberry sauce

Serves 8

thinly pared rind and juice
of 1 lemon

thinly pared rind and juice
of 1 orange

12 oz/350 g cranberries,
thawed, if frozen

¾ cup superfine sugar

2 tbsp arrowroot, mixed
with 3 tbsp cold water

Cut the strips of lemon and orange rind into thin shreds and place in a heavy-bottom pan. If using fresh cranberries, rinse well and remove any stalks. Add the berries, citrus juice, and sugar to the pan and cook over medium heat, stirring occasionally, for 5 minutes, or until the berries begin to burst.

Strain the juice into a clean pan and reserve the cranberries. Stir the arrowroot mixture into the juice, then bring to a boil, stirring continuously, until the sauce is smooth and thickened. Remove from the heat and stir in the reserved cranberries.

Transfer the cranberry sauce to a bowl and let cool, then cover with plastic wrap and chill in the refrigerator.

Chicken fajitas

Serves 4

4 skinless, boneless chicken breasts

2 red bell peppers, seeded and cut into 1-inch/2.5-cm strips

Marinade

3 tbsp olive oil, plus extra for drizzling

3 tbsp maple syrup or honey

1 tbsp red wine vinegar

2 garlic cloves, crushed

2 tsp dried oregano

1–2 tsp dried red pepper flakes

salt and pepper

To serve

8 flour tortillas, warmed

guacamole

sour cream

bottled salsa

shredded iceberg lettuce

To make the marinade, place the oil, maple syrup, vinegar, garlic, oregano, pepper flakes, and salt and pepper to taste in a large, shallow dish or bowl and mix together.

Slice the chicken across the grain into slices 1 inch/2.5 cm thick. Toss in the marinade until well coated. Cover and let chill in the refrigerator for 2–3 hours, turning occasionally.

Heat a grill pan until hot. Lift the chicken slices from the marinade with a slotted spoon, lay them on the pan, and cook over medium–high heat for 3–4 minutes on each side until cooked through. Transfer the chicken to a warmed serving plate and keep warm.

Add the bell peppers, skin side down, to the pan and cook for 2 minutes on each side. Transfer to the serving plate.

Pile the cooked chicken and bell peppers onto the warmed tortillas, along with some guacamole, sour cream, salsa, and shredded lettuce.

Italian turkey steaks

Serves 4

1 tbsp olive oil

4 turkey scallops or steaks

2 red bell peppers

1 red onion

2 garlic cloves, finely chopped

1¼ cups strained tomatoes

⅔ cup medium white wine

1 tbsp chopped fresh marjoram

salt and pepper

14 oz/400 g canned cannellini beans, drained and rinsed

3 tbsp fresh white breadcrumbs

fresh basil sprigs, to garnish

Heat the oil in a flameproof casserole or heavy-bottom skillet. Add the turkey scallops and cook over medium heat for 5–10 minutes, turning occasionally, until golden. Transfer to a plate.

Seed and slice the red bell peppers. Slice the onion, add to the skillet with the bell peppers, and cook over low heat, stirring occasionally, for 5 minutes, or until softened. Add the garlic and cook for an additional 2 minutes. Return the turkey to the skillet and add the strained tomatoes, wine, and marjoram. Season to taste. Bring to a boil, then reduce the heat, cover, and simmer, stirring occasionally, for 25–30 minutes, or until the turkey is cooked through and tender.

Stir in the cannellini beans. Simmer for an additional 5 minutes. Sprinkle the breadcrumbs over the top and place under a preheated medium–hot broiler for 2–3 minutes, or until golden. Serve, garnished with basil.

My special recipes

....

....

....

....

....

....

....

....

....

....

....

....

....

....

Notes ....

....

....

....

....

My special recipes

....

....

....

....

....

....

....

....

....

....

....

....

....

....

Notes ....

....

....

....

....

My special recipes

....

....

....

....

....

....

....

....

....

....

....

....

....

....

Notes ....

....

....

....

....

My special recipes

....

....

....

....

....

....

....

....

....

....

....

....

....

....

Notes ....

....

....

....

....

My special recipes

....

....

....

....

....

....

....

....

....

....

....

....

....

....

Notes ....

....

....

....

....

My special recipes

....

....

....

....

....

....

....

....

....

....

....

....

....

....

Notes ....

....

....

....

....

Fish & seafood

Buying and storing fish & shellfish

Buying

Freshness is the all-important factor to consider when buying any seafood that hasn't been preserved. Fresh fish is highly perishable so, unless you have access to supplies as they are landed, much of the "fresh" fish available will have been frozen on the fishing vessel and then thawed. It is vitally important for you to know the signs of fish in prime condition and those specimens that you should avoid.

Wherever you buy your seafood, the display slab should be spotlessly clean and there should be plenty of crushed ice around the seafood. Whole, cleaned fish deteriorate less quickly than steaks or fillets, so look for a display that includes these.

Good-quality fish has a fresh, ocean-like aroma. It shouldn't smell "fishy." If there is any whiff of ammonia or unpleasantness, don't buy. Whole fish should be firm, not floppy, and the flesh should feel firm and elastic when you press gently. The eyes should be protruding and clear, not sunken or cloudy; any scales should be shiny and tight against the skin; the gills should be clear and bright red, not dull or gray. Fillets and steaks should be cleanly cut and look moist and fresh, with a shiny "bloom" on the surface and no yellowing or browning.

Never buy packaged fish with damaged packaging. There should not be much air between the fish and the wrapping or any pools of liquid or blood. And, of course, you should always check the expiration date.

The term "shellfish" includes bivalves (clams, mussels, oysters, scallops), crustaceans (crabs, lobsters, shrimp), and cephalopods (squid and octopus). Shellfish should all be consumed on the day of purchase.

When clams, mussels, and oysters are sold alive, the shells should be tightly closed; if open shells don't snap shut when tapped, they are dead. They should be in a net or porous bag (not a plastic bag). Most scallops are sold shucked, often with the roe attached, but occasionally in the shell. Shrimp are often sold frozen, but can be raw or cooked. It is best to buy them in the shell—look for firm flesh, and avoid any with black spots on the shells (except in the case of large black jumbo shrimp). Squid and octopus are sold fresh and frozen—the flesh should have no brown patches. Both smell foul if not fresh. Make sure the packaging on sealed, smoked seafood isn't damaged and that the expiration date hasn't expired. If buying loose seafood, it shouldn't have an unpleasant smell or dry edges. If salt cod is still flexible when you buy it, wrap it in a damp towel and chill for up to three weeks; if it is rigid, wrap it in foil and chill for up to three months. Check the expiration dates on canned seafood.

Safe storage

Get your purchase home and refrigerated as soon as possible, ideally transporting it in an insulated bag. Remove all packaging and clean the fish with a damp cloth, then wrap it in wet paper towels and place on a lipped plate at the bottom of the refrigerator, at a temperature no higher than 40°F/4°C. Keep live clams, mussels, and oysters in their bag. Do not put them in a bowl of water or a sealed container, because they will die. Store oysters in their shells, rounded cup down, covered with a wet cloth or some seaweed.

All shellfish should be stored in the bottom of the refrigerator and cooked or eaten within 12 hours. Fresh fish should also be cooked and eaten on the day of purchase, although most remain edible for another day if properly refrigerated. Oily fish spoils more quickly than white fish.

Refrigerate smoked or marinated seafood as soon as you get it home, and consume within two or three days, or by the expiration date.

Ways to cook fish

The Canadian Cooking Theory, developed some decades ago, advocates cooking fish for 10 minutes per 1 inch/2.5 cm at the thickest part for dry-heat methods. This is an easy approach for anyone new to seafood cooking, but many chefs today prefer 8–9 minutes for slightly less well-cooked fish. This is a matter of personal taste, so experiment and know how to tell when fish is cooked as you enjoy it: perfectly cooked fish is opaque with milky white juices and flakes and comes away from the bone easily; undercooked fish resists flaking, is translucent, and has clear juices; overcooked fish looks dry and falls apart into thin pieces. Tuna and other meaty fish can be roasted and pan-seared like beef to be served rare, medium, and well-done. When charbroiling, sautéing, pan-, and stir-frying, start with a well-heated pan or wok, so that the fish develops a crust that retains internal moisture.

Dry-heat cooking—grilling, broiling, charbroiling, and roasting

These are good methods for cooking whole fish, fillets, steaks, and kebabs. Oily fish are well suited to broiling, grilling, and charbroiling, because their natural oils baste the flesh and their flavors are not overpowered by smoky aromas. Marinate white fish before grilling. Grilling and broiling are similar, with the former cooking from the bottom and the latter from the top. In both cases, position the rack about 4 inches/10 cm from the heat. Brush the rack with oil, add the fish, and cook until the flesh flakes easily, basting with a marinade or melted butter. Ideally cook without turning; if the surface is browning too quickly, adjust the rack position. Grill thin fillets and small fish, such as sardines, in a hinged fish basket.

Charbroiling is a quick way to give fish a grill flavor without having to light a grill. Heat a cast-iron grill pan over high heat, brush the fish with oil, and charbroil until seared on one side and cooked through. Whole fish are particularly delicious when roasted. Preheat the oven to 450°F/230°C and make a few slashes on each side. Rub the fish with oil, put in a roasting pan, and roast, uncovered, until the flesh comes away from the bone when tested—the skin becomes crisp, while the flesh remains tenderly moist.

Wet-heat cooking—poaching, steaming, and stewing

Fish is excellent poached or steamed. Although these techniques are very easy, they can still overcook fish, so pay close attention. Another advantage is that the cooking liquid can be incorporated into a tasty sauce to accompany the fish. Poach in gently simmering liquid flavored with lemon and herbs for 8–12 minutes per 1 inch/2.5 cm of thickness. When steaming, make sure the seasoned fish never actually touches the water. Steam, covered, for 3–5 minutes for fillets and steaks, and 8–9 minutes per 1 inch/2.5 cm of thickness for whole fish. Seafish stews often contain a variety of fish, simmered with other ingredients. To prevent overcooking, add the fish toward the end, adding the most delicate pieces last—they will take only 2–3 minutes. Don't let the liquid boil.

Cooking in oil—sautéing, stir-frying, and pan- and deep-frying

Fish steaks and fillets are most suited to these quick techniques. For sautéing and pan-frying, heat 1/4 inch/5 mm vegetable oil in a hot sauté or skillet, dust the fish with seasoned flour, and fry over medium–high heat for 2–3 minutes on each side for thin fillets, and up to 5–6 minutes for steaks 1 inch/2.5 cm thick. Deep-frying requires fish to be coated in batter or crumbs and for the oil to be maintained at a steady 350°F/180°C. If you don't have a deep-fat fryer with a controlled thermostat, use a deep, heavy-bottom pan and a thermometer: if the oil is too cool, the fried fish will be soggy; if it is too hot, the outside will be overcooked while the center will still be raw. Work in batches to prevent overcrowding and a reduction in the oil's temperature.

Roasted salmon

Serves 4

6 tbsp extra virgin olive oil

1 onion, sliced

1 leek, trimmed and sliced

juice of ½ lemon

2 tbsp chopped fresh parsley

2 tbsp chopped fresh dill

1 lb 2 oz/500 g salmon fillets

salt and pepper

freshly cooked baby spinach leaves
and lemon wedges, to serve

Preheat the oven to 400°F/200°C. Heat 1 tablespoon of the oil in a skillet over medium heat. Add the onion and leek and cook, stirring, for about 4 minutes until slightly softened.

Meanwhile, put the remaining oil in a small bowl with the lemon juice and herbs, and season with salt and pepper. Stir together well. Rinse the fish under cold running water, then pat dry with paper towels. Arrange the fish in a shallow, ovenproof baking dish.

Remove the skillet from the heat and spread the onion and leek over the fish. Pour the oil mixture over the top, ensuring that everything is well coated. Roast in the center of the preheated oven for about 10 minutes or until the fish is cooked through.

Arrange the cooked spinach on warmed serving plates. Remove the fish and vegetables from the oven and arrange on top of the spinach. Serve immediately, accompanied by the lemon wedges.

Tuna with green sauce

Serves 4

4 fresh tuna steaks, about
¾ inch/2 cm thick

olive oil, for brushing

salt and pepper

Green sauce

2 oz/55 g fresh flat-leaf parsley,
leaves and stems

4 scallions, chopped

2 garlic cloves, chopped

3 anchovy fillets in oil, drained

1 oz/30 g fresh basil leaves

½ tbsp capers in brine, rinsed and
dried

2 sprigs fresh oregano or ½ tsp
dried oregano

½ cup extra virgin olive oil

1–2 tbsp lemon juice, to taste

To make the Green Sauce, put the parsley, scallions, garlic, anchovy fillets, basil, capers, and oregano in a food processor. Pulse to chop and blend together. With the motor still running, pour in the oil through the feed tube. Add lemon juice to taste, then whiz again. If the sauce is too thick, add a little extra oil. Cover and chill until required.

Place a cast-iron grill pan over high heat until you can feel the heat rising from the surface. Brush the tuna steaks with oil and place, oiled-side down, on the hot pan and cook for 2 minutes.

Lightly brush the top side of the tuna steaks with a little more oil. Use a pair of tongs to turn over the tuna steaks, then season with salt and pepper to taste. Continue cooking the steaks for an additional 2 minutes for rare or up to 4 minutes for well-done.

Transfer the tuna steaks to serving plates and serve with the Green Sauce spooned over.

Grilled swordfish with cilantro & lime butter

Serves 4

corn oil, for brushing

4 swordfish steaks, each about
6 oz/175 g and 1 inch/2.5 cm thick

salt and pepper

fresh cilantro leaves, to garnish

Cilantro & lime butter

2/3 cup unsalted butter, softened

finely grated rind of 1 large lime

1/4 tsp freshly squeezed lime juice

1 tbsp very finely shredded
cilantro leaves

pinch of ground cumin

To make the Cilantro & Lime butter, put the butter into a bowl and beat until it is soft and smooth. Stir in the lime rind, lime juice, shredded cilantro, cumin, and salt and pepper to taste. Spoon the butter onto a piece of wax paper and roll into a log about 1¼ inches/3 cm thick. Refrigerate for at least 45 minutes or freeze until required.

When you are ready to cook the swordfish steaks, preheat the broiler to high. Brush the broiler rack with a little oil and position it about 4 inches/10 cm below the heat source.

Brush the steaks with oil and season with salt and pepper to taste. Put the steaks onto the broiler rack and cook for 4 minutes. Turn them over, then brush with a little more oil, season with salt and pepper to taste, and cook for an additional 4–5 minutes, or until the fish is cooked and the flesh flakes easily.

Meanwhile, cut the butter into 8 equal slices. Put 2 slices of the butter on top of each steak and serve at once, garnished with cilantro leaves.

Flaky pastry fish pie

Serves 6

1 lb 7 oz/650 g white fish fillets, such as cod or haddock, skinned

1¼ cups milk

1 bay leaf

4 peppercorns

1 small onion, finely sliced

3 tbsp butter, plus extra for greasing

⅔ cup all-purpose flour, plus extra for dusting

1 tbsp chopped fresh parsley or tarragon

⅔ cup light cream

2 hard-cooked eggs, roughly chopped

14 oz/400 g prepared puff pastry

1 egg, beaten

salt and pepper

Preheat the oven to 400°F/200°C. Grease a 2-pint/1.2-liter pie plate. Put the fish in a skillet and cover with the milk. Add the bay leaf, peppercorns, and onion slices. Bring to a boil, then reduce the heat and simmer gently for 10–12 minutes. Remove from the heat and strain the milk into a measuring cup. Add the remaining milk. Flake the fish into large pieces.

Melt the butter in a pan over low heat, add the flour, and cook, stirring continuously, for 2–3 minutes. Remove from the heat and gradually stir in the reserved milk, beating well after each addition. Return to the heat and cook, stirring until thick, smooth, and glossy. Add the herbs, cream, and salt and pepper to taste.

Put the fish in the pie plate, add the hard-cooked eggs, and season with salt and pepper to taste. Pour the sauce over the fish and mix carefully.

Roll out the pastry on a lightly floured counter until just larger than the pie plate. Cut off a strip ½ inch/1 cm wide from around the edge. Moisten the rim of the dish with water and press the pastry strip onto it. Moisten the pastry collar and put on the pastry lid. Crimp the edges to seal well. Brush with the beaten egg. Put the pie on a baking tray and bake near the top of the preheated oven for 20–25 minutes. Remove from the oven and serve immediately.

Calamares

Serves 6

1 lb/450 g prepared squid

all-purpose flour, for coating

sunflower oil, for deep-frying

salt

lemon wedges, to garnish

aïoli, to serve

Slice the squid into ½-inch/1-cm rings and halve the tentacles if large. Rinse under cold running water and dry well with paper towels. Dust the squid rings with flour so that they are lightly coated.

Heat the oil in a deep-fat fryer, large, heavy-bottom pan, or wok to 350–375°F/180–190°C, or until a cube of bread browns in 30 seconds. Deep-fry the squid rings in small batches for 2–3 minutes, or until golden brown and crisp all over, turning several times (if you deep-fry too many squid rings at one time, the oil temperature will drop and they will be soggy). Do not overcook because the squid will become tough and rubbery instead of moist and tender.

Remove with a slotted spoon and drain well on paper towels. Keep warm in a low oven while you deep-fry the remaining squid rings.

Sprinkle the fried squid rings with salt and serve piping hot, garnished with lemon wedges for squeezing over. Accompany with a bowl of aïoli for dipping.

Crab cakes

Makes 16

1 potato, peeled and cut into chunks

pinch of salt

4 scallions, chopped

1 garlic clove, chopped

1 tbsp chopped fresh thyme

1 tbsp chopped fresh basil

1 tbsp chopped fresh cilantro

8 oz/225 g white crabmeat, drained, if canned, and thawed, if frozen

½ tsp Dijon mustard

½ fresh green chile, seeded and finely chopped

1 egg, lightly beaten

all-purpose flour, for dusting

sunflower oil, for pan-frying

pepper

lime wedges, to garnish

dip or salsa of your choice, to serve

Put the potato in a small pan and add water to cover. Add the salt. Bring to a boil, reduce the heat, cover, and let simmer for 10–15 minutes until softened. Drain well, turn into a large bowl, and mash with a potato masher or fork until smooth.

Meanwhile, put the scallions, garlic, thyme, basil, and cilantro in a mortar and pound with a pestle until smooth. Add the herb paste to the mashed potato with the crabmeat, mustard, chile, egg, and pepper to taste. Mix well, cover with plastic wrap, and let chill in the refrigerator for 30 minutes.

Sprinkle flour onto a large, flat plate. Shape spoonfuls of the crabmeat mixture into small balls with your hands, then flatten slightly and dust with flour, shaking off any excess. Heat the oil in a skillet over high heat, add the crab cakes, and cook in batches for 2–3 minutes on each side until golden. Remove with a slotted spoon and drain on paper towels. Set aside to cool to room temperature.

Arrange the crab cakes on a serving dish and garnish with lime wedges. Serve with a bowl of dip or salsa.

My special recipes

....

....

....

....

....

....

....

....

....

....

....

....

....

Notes ....

....

....

....

....

My special recipes

....

....

....

....

....

....

....

....

....

....

....

....

....

....

Notes ....

....

....

....

....

My special recipes

....

....

....

....

....

....

....

....

....

....

....

....

....

....

Notes ....

....

....

....

....

My special recipes

....

....

....

....

....

....

....

....

....

....

....

....

....

....

Notes ....

....

....

....

....

My special recipes

....

....

....

....

....

....

....

....

....

....

....

....

....

....

Notes ....

....

....

....

....

My special recipes

....

....

....

....

....

....

....

....

....

....

....

....

....

....

....

Notes ....

....

....

....

....

Chapter Content

Sweet & baked

Getting started

EQUIPMENT

Measuring cups, mixing bowls, a wooden spoon, a few baking pans, and a rolling pin are all the items you need to begin baking. But as the baking bug bites, you can gradually add other tools to those basics, such as an electric mixer, which, although not essential, will certainly make the job easier and quicker.

Measuring

For successful baking, it is essential to have accurate measuring scales or cups and a set of measuring spoons. Electronic or balance scales are more accurate than measuring cups, which measure ingredients by volume. If you intend to do a lot of baking but generally use cups for measuring, it is worth investing in a set of scales to ensure success every time. It is important to bear in mind that spoon measures are always level unless otherwise stated in the recipe.

Mixing, Beating, and Blending

Bowls: You will need a selection of bowls of various sizes. Choose from ceramic, glass, or stainless steel.
Spoons: Wooden spoons in a variety of sizes are essential for beating ingredients together. A large metal spoon is useful for folding in flour.
Spatulas: Plastic or silicone spatulas are ideal for scraping out bowls with the minimum of waste, as well as for folding in flour.

Whisks and Mixers: Electric appliances take the hard work out of creaming and whisking cake batters. A hand-held electric mixer is sufficient for cakes, while a freestanding mixer is useful for those who like to bake in larger quantities and for making bread. A manual wire whisk is good for whisking egg whites and for whisked sponge mixes if you don't have or don't want to buy an electric mixer.
Food Processors: These are great for rubbing fat into flour quickly and efficiently. They can also be used to prepare cake batters, but tend not to incorporate as much air as mixing by hand or with a whisk, so the resulting cakes may be more dense.

Bakeware

It is advisable to invest in a few good-quality baking pans. If looked after, they will last a lifetime, and they are less likely than inexpensive pans to twist or buckle in the oven and to cause sticking or burning. Choose ones that feel relatively heavy and do not bend easily.
The most useful to begin with are:
• Cookie sheets
• 7-inch/18-cm shallow cake pans
• 8-inch/20-cm shallow cake pans
• 9-inch/23-cm shallow cake pans
• 8-inch/20-cm deep loose-bottom pan
• 8-inch/20-cm square cake pan
• 8 x 4 x 2-inch/20 x 10 x 5-cm and 9 x 5 x 3-inch/23 x 13 x 8 cm loaf pans
• 12-hole muffin pans
• Jelly roll pan
• 8-inch/20-cm tart pan

INGREDIENTS

Flour

Wheat flour is the most commonly used flour for baking. The amount of gluten (protein) in wheat flour varies between the different types: All-purpose flour has the bran and wheat germ removed, and is then fortified with vitamins. Soft all-purpose flour is made from wheat with a low gluten content. It has a fine texture and is ideal for making cakes, pie dough, and cookies. White bread flour is milled from wheat with a high gluten content and is used for breads and most yeast cooking. Self-rising flour is all-purpose white flour with baking powder added as a raising agent. To make self-rising flour add 2 teaspoons of baking powder to each scant $1^5/_8$ cups all-purpose flour. Whole wheat flour is flour that has been milled from the whole of the wheat grain. It is coarser and heavier than white flour. It is available as a strong (high-gluten) flour for bread making and a soft (lower-gluten) flour for cakes and pastry.
Other flours such as brown flour, malted flour, corn flour, and buckwheat, rye, rice, and chestnut flours are also sometimes used to a limited extent in baking, each with its own unique characteristic or flavor.

Sugars

Most sugar is produced from one of two sources: sugar cane or sugar beet. There are a number of different types of sugar, each with its own particular qualities. Unrefined sugars are made from sugar cane and have a higher mineral, vitamin, and trace element content than refined sugars.

Granulated sugar can be used to achieve a crunchy texture in some cookies and in cakes prepared by the rubbing-in method.

Superfine sugar has a finer crystal and dissolves more readily. It is the type of sugar most frequently used in baking. Because it dissolves readily it is perfect for making meringues. It can be substituted for granulated sugar cup for cup.

Golden granulated sugar, golden superfine, and golden confectioners' sugar are unrefined forms of the refined sugars.

Molasses sugar is a dark, fine-grained unrefined sugar from Mauritius that is used for rich fruit cakes. This unique sugar contains the highest amount of natural molasses of any sugar, resulting in an extra rich flavor and moistness. Molasses syrup is the dark-colored syrup that is left over after sugar has been refined. It is very concentrated, so only a small amount is required. Store molasses in tightly sealed containers at room temperature or in the refrigerator.

Raw brown sugar is a large, coarse-grained brown sugar that can be made from either refined or unrefined sugar. As well as being used in baking, it is sometimes sprinkled over the tops of pies, crumbles, and cakes for its crunchy texture.

Light and dark brown sugars are usually refined light and dark muscovado sugars. They are usually refined white sugar tossed in molasses or syrup.

Confectioners' sugar, sometimes called powdered sugar, is fine and powdery and dissolves almost instantly. It is used in cookies and pastry, and in frostings and fillings.

Fats

Butter produces the best flavor. Unsalted butter is generally considered best for baking. If you do use salted butter, you will not need to add any extra salt to the recipe (except for bread making).

Use butter straight from the refrigerator when making pastry and at room temperature when making cakes.

Margarine is preferred by some people for baking. Block margarine is generally the best to use, but soft margarine is needed when making cakes by the all-in-one method.

Low-fat spreads are not suitable for baking, because they contain a high proportion of water.

Lard is made from pork fat or from solidified vegetable oils.

Shortening and white vegetable fat have a bland flavor, but give a light, short texture to pastry and cookies. They are usually combined with butter for flavor.

Eggs

The size of eggs used in baking is important. Store eggs in the refrigerator away from strong-smelling foods. Remove from the refrigerator to return to room temperature before using if possible, because cold eggs do not combine as well with other ingredients or trap as much air.

Raising agents

Baking powder is a mixture of cream of tartar and baking soda. When mixed with moisture, it releases carbon dioxide, a harmless gas that expands during baking to make the food rise.

Baking soda produces carbon dioxide when mixed with an acid such as lemon juice or buttermilk. It should always be mixed with other dry ingredients before the liquid is added.

Yeast is a single-cell organism that converts the natural sugars in flour to produce carbon dioxide. Yeast needs warmth, moisture, and food (sugars) to work. It is available in both dried and fresh forms for baking.

Baking tips

Greasing and lining cake pans

Unless you have nonstick bakeware, you will need to grease your baking pans before using, and you may prefer to take the extra precaution of greasing nonstick pans in any case. A little butter or margarine can be smeared onto the pan, or a light-flavored oil can be brushed over the entire inside surface with a pastry brush to give a very light coating.

Some recipes require the baking pan to be lined. In some cases, only the bottom of the pan needs to be lined, which helps to ensure that the cake is successfully turned out. Use wax paper or nonstick parchment paper to line the pans.

Lining a round cake pan: Place the pan on the paper and draw around it. Cut out the circle just inside the drawn line. Cut a strip of paper about $^3/_4$ inch/2 cm wider than the depth of the pan and long enough to go around the pan. Fold over about $^1/_2$ inch/1 cm along one long edge and snip from the edge up to the fold at $^3/_4$-inch/2-cm intervals along the length. Lightly grease the pan and position the strip of paper around the edge so that the snipped edge lies flat on the bottom of the pan. Lay the disc of paper in the bottom and lightly grease.

For rich fruit cakes, extra protection is needed to prevent the edges from burning or drying out during the extended cooking time. Line the pan as above, but use a double thickness of paper. Cut a double-thickness strip of brown paper about $^3/_4$ inch/2 cm deeper than the pan. Wrap around the outside of the pan and secure with string.

Lining a shallow or jelly roll pan: Cut the paper about 3 inches/7.5 cm longer and wider than the pan. Lightly grease the pan and place the paper on top. Snip at the corners and press into the pan. Lightly grease the paper.

Lining a loaf pan: Lightly grease the pan. Cut two strips of paper, one the width of the pan and long enough to cover the sides and bottom, and one the length of the pan and long enough to cover the bottom and sides. Press each piece into place and lightly grease.

Is it cooked?

Follow the timings in the recipe as a guideline, but also rely on your own judgment, because ovens vary in temperature. Small cakes should be well risen, firm, and springy to the touch, and sponge cakes should also be springy to the touch.

Test by gently pressing the cake with a finger. Once you have removed your finger, the cake should spring back, but if you can still see the fingerprint, return the cake to the oven for a few minutes longer. Fruit cake and deep sponge cakes are best tested with a skewer inserted into the center. The skewer should come out clean when the cake is cooked.

For most cakes, let cool for a few minutes in the pan before turning out and transferring to a wire rack to cool completely. Some cakes, such as rich fruit cakes, benefit from being allowed to cool completely in the pan.

Baking blind

When used to line a pan, a pastry shell is often precooked to set the pastry before the filling is added.

Line the pan with the rolled-out pastry and prick the bottom with a fork. Chill for about 30 minutes in the refrigerator or 10 minutes in the freezer (you can also bake pastry shells blind from frozen). Line the pastry shell with a sheet of nonstick baking paper, wax paper, or foil and fill with ceramic or metal pie weights or dried beans or rice. Bake for 10 minutes, then remove the paper and weights and bake for an additional 10 minutes until the pastry is just golden. Remove from the oven and brush a little beaten egg or egg white over the bottom to seal.

What went wrong?

Accurate measuring and careful following of the recipe should ensure success. However, when things do go wrong, there is often a simple reason, and if you identify the cause, the mistake can be avoided in the future.

CAKES

Sunk in the middle
- Cake slightly undercooked
- Oven door opened too early
- Batter too wet
- Overbeating of the fat and sugar
- Too much raising agent
- Oven temperature too low

Uneven rise
- Batter not spread evenly
- Flour not folded in evenly (whisked sponges)
- Oven not properly preheated
- Oven or oven shelves not level

Peaked or cracked top
- Baking in too hot an oven
- Too much batter in the pan
- Too much raising agent
- Batter too wet or too dry
- Cooking too near the top of the oven (cooking the crust too quickly)

Crust too pale
- Cake cooked too low in the oven
- Oven overloaded
- Oven temperature too low

Crust too dark
- Cake cooked too near the top of the oven
- Oven temperature too high
- Pan too large
- Baked too long

Speckled top
- Insufficient beating of the fat with the sugar
- Granulated or raw brown sugar used

SHORTCRUST PASTRY

Difficult to roll
- Too dry
- Self-rising flour used instead of all-purpose flour
- Too much fat
- Overmixed

Excessive shrinking
- Overhandling
- Dough stretched when rolling
- Not allowing dough to rest before baking

Soggy pastry
- Not fully cooked
- Too much liquid
- Pie cover placed over hot filling
- No vent for steam to escape (pies)
- Filling poured into pastry shell that has cracks or holes in

Hard or tough pastry
- Overhandling
- Too little fat
- Too much liquid
- Oven temperature too low

Blistered crust
- Water not evenly mixed in
- Fat not properly rubbed in
- Insufficient beating
- Oven temperature too low

BREAD

Insufficiently risen
- Too little yeast
- Too little sugar
- Too much salt
- Yeast out of date
- Insufficient time proving
- Proving at too low a temperature

Bread risen too much
- Too much yeast
- Too little salt

Sunk in the center
- Too much liquid
- Too little salt
- Too much yeast
- Too much proving

Center soggy
- Too much of the wet ingredients/water
- Oven temperature too high

Damp crust
- Left in the pan too long after baking
- Wrapped while warm

Crust too dark
- Too much sugar
- Cooked too long or at too high a temperature

Dense texture
- Not enough liquid
- Soft flour used
- Insufficient kneading
- Too much salt
- Liquid too hot (kills the yeast)
- Grains without sufficient gluten used

Coarse, open texture
- Too much liquid
- Too much proving
- Oven temperature too low

Flat top
- Flour too soft
- Dough too wet

Victoria sandwich

Makes 8–10 slices

¾ cup butter, at room temperature, plus extra for greasing

scant 1 cup superfine sugar

3 eggs, beaten

scant 1¼ cups self-rising flour

pinch of salt

3 tbsp raspberry jam

1 tbsp superfine or confectioners' sugar

Preheat the oven to 350°F/180°C. Grease two 8-inch/20-cm round shallow cake pans and line the bottom with wax or nonstick parchment paper.

Cream the butter and sugar together in a bowl until pale and fluffy. Add the eggs, a little at a time, beating well after each addition.

Sift the flour and salt together, then gently fold into the mixture using a metal spoon or a spatula. Divide the batter evenly among the prepared pans and smooth the surfaces.

Bake both cakes on the same shelf in the center of the preheated oven for 25–30 minutes until well risen, golden brown, and beginning to shrink from the side of each pan.

Let stand in the pans for 1 minute. Using a palette knife, loosen the cakes from around the edge of each pan. Turn out the cakes onto a clean dish towel, remove the lining paper, and invert onto a wire rack (this prevents the rack from marking the top of the cakes).

When completely cool, sandwich together with the raspberry jam and sprinkle with the sugar. The cake is delicious when freshly baked, but any remaining cake can be stored in an airtight container for up to 1 week.

Mississippi mud pie

Serves 8

Pie dough

1½ cups all-purpose flour, plus extra for dusting

2 tbsp unsweetened cocoa

generous ½ cup unsalted butter

2 tbsp superfine sugar

1–2 tbsp cold water

Filling

¾ cup unsalted butter

scant 1¾ cups packed brown sugar

4 eggs, lightly beaten

4 tbsp unsweetened cocoa, sifted

5½ oz/150 g semisweet chocolate

1¼ cups light cream

1 tsp chocolate extract

To decorate

scant 2 cups heavy cream, whipped

chocolate flakes

chocolate curls

To make the pie dough, sift the flour and cocoa into a mixing bowl. Rub in the butter with your fingertips until the mixture resembles fine breadcrumbs. Stir in the sugar and enough cold water to mix to a soft dough. Wrap the dough in plastic wrap and let chill in the refrigerator for 15 minutes.

Preheat the oven to 375°F/190°C. Roll out the dough on a lightly floured counter and use to line a 9-inch/23-cm loose-bottom tart pan or ceramic pie plate. Line with parchment paper and fill with pie weights. Bake in the oven for 15 minutes. Remove from the oven and take out the paper and beans. Bake the pie shell for an additional 10 minutes.

To make the filling, beat the butter and sugar together in a bowl and gradually beat in the eggs with the cocoa. Melt the chocolate in a heatproof bowl set over a saucepan of gently simmering water, then beat it into the mixture with the light cream and the chocolate extract.

Reduce the oven temperature to 325°F/160°C. Pour the mixture into the pie shell and bake for 45 minutes, or until the filling has set gently.

Let the mud pie cool completely, then transfer it to a serving plate. Cover with the whipped cream.

Scatter over the chocolate flakes and chocolate curls and then let chill until ready to serve.

Traditional apple pie

Serves 6

Pie dough

generous 2³⁄₈ cups all-purpose flour

pinch of salt

4¹⁄₂ tbsp butter or margarine, cut into small pieces

scant ¹⁄₂ cup lard or vegetable shortening, cut into small pieces

about 6 tbsp cold water

beaten egg or milk, for glazing

Filling

1 lb 10 oz–2 lb 4 oz/750 g–1 kg cooking apples, peeled, cored, and sliced

scant ²⁄₃ cup packed brown or superfine sugar, plus extra for sprinkling

¹⁄₂–1 tsp ground cinnamon, allspice, or ground ginger

1–2 tbsp water (optional)

To make the pie dough, sift the flour and salt into a large bowl. Add the butter and fat and rub in with the fingertips until the mixture resembles fine breadcrumbs. Add the water and gather the mixture together into a dough. Wrap the dough and let chill in the refrigerator for 30 minutes.

Preheat the oven to 425°F/220°C. Roll out almost two thirds of the pie dough thinly and use to line a deep 9-inch/23-cm pie plate.

Mix the apples with the sugar and spice and pack into the pastry shell; the filling can come up above the rim. Add the water if needed, particularly if the apples are a dry variety.

Roll out the remaining pie dough to form a lid. Dampen the edges of the pie rim with water and position the lid, pressing the edges firmly together. Trim and crimp the edges.

Use the trimmings to cut out leaves or other shapes to decorate the top of the pie, dampen, and attach. Glaze the top of the pie with beaten egg or milk, make 1–2 slits in the top, and place the pie on a baking sheet.

Bake in the preheated oven for 20 minutes, then reduce the temperature to 350°F/180°C and bake for an additional 30 minutes, or until the pastry is a light golden brown. Serve hot or cold, sprinkled with sugar.

Double chocolate chip cookies

Makes 24

½ cup unsalted butter, softened, plus extra for greasing

¼ cup granulated sugar

¼ cup light brown sugar

1 egg, beaten

½ tsp vanilla extract

¾ cup all-purpose flour

2 tbsp unsweetened cocoa

½ tsp baking soda

⅔ cup milk chocolate chips

½ cup walnuts, coarsely chopped

Preheat the oven to 350°F/180°C, then grease 3 cookie sheets. Place the butter, granulated sugar, and brown sugar in a bowl and beat until light and fluffy.

Gradually beat in the egg and vanilla extract.

Sift the flour, cocoa, and baking soda into the mixture and stir in carefully. Stir in the chocolate chips and walnuts. Drop tablespoonfuls of the mixture onto the prepared cookie sheets, spaced well apart to allow for spreading.

Bake in the oven for 10–15 minutes, or until the mixture has spread and the cookies are beginning to feel firm. Remove from the oven and let cool on the cookie sheets for 2 minutes, before transferring to wire racks.

Scones

Makes 10–12

4 tbsp butter, diced and chilled, plus extra for greasing

3½ cups all-purpose flour, plus extra for dusting

½ tsp salt

2 tsp baking powder

2 tbsp superfine sugar

generous 1 cup milk, plus extra for glazing

whipped cream and strawberry jam, to serve

Preheat the oven to 425°F/220°C. Grease a cookie sheet.

Sift the flour, salt, and baking powder together into a bowl. Rub in the butter with your fingertips until the mixture resembles fine breadcrumbs. Stir in the sugar. Make a well in the center and pour in the milk. Quickly mix with a round-bladed knife to form a soft dough.

Turn out the dough onto a lightly floured counter and knead lightly. Roll out to a thickness of about ½ inch/1 cm. Don't be heavy-handed—scones need a light touch. Using a plain 2½-inch/6-cm cookie cutter, cut out 10–12 circles and transfer to the prepared cookie sheet.

Brush with the milk to glaze and bake in the preheated oven for 10–12 minutes until well risen and golden.

Transfer to a wire rack and let cool. Split the scones and serve with the cream and the strawberry jam.

New York cheesecake

Serves 8–10

sunflower oil, for brushing
6 tbsp butter
2⅓ cups crushed graham crackers
1¾ cups cream cheese
2 large eggs
¾ cup superfine sugar
1½ tsp vanilla extract
2 cups sour cream

Topping
¼ cup superfine sugar
4 tbsp water
2 cups fresh blueberries
1 tsp arrowroot

Preheat the oven to 375°F/190°C. Brush an 8-inch/20-cm springform pan with oil. Melt the butter in a pan over low heat. Stir in the crackers, then spread the mixture over the bottom of the pan. Place the cream cheese, eggs, ½ cup of the sugar, and ½ teaspoon of the vanilla extract in a food processor. Process until smooth. Pour over the cracker base and smooth the top. Place on a baking tray and bake for 20 minutes until set. Remove from the oven and set aside for 20 minutes. Do not turn off the oven.

Mix the cream with the remaining sugar and vanilla extract in a bowl. Spoon over the cheesecake. Return to the oven for 10 minutes, let cool, then cover with plastic wrap and chill in the refrigerator for 8 hours, or overnight.

To make the topping, place the sugar in a pan with 2 tablespoons of the water over low heat and stir until the sugar has dissolved. Increase the heat, add the blueberries, cover, and cook for a few minutes, or until they begin to soften. Remove from the heat. Mix the arrowroot with the remaining water in a bowl, add to the blueberries, and stir until smooth. Return to low heat. Cook until the juice thickens and turns translucent. Let cool.

Remove the cheesecake from the pan 1 hour before serving. Spoon over the topping and chill until ready to serve.

White bread

Makes 1 large loaf or 8 rolls

butter, for greasing

3¼ cups white bread flour, plus extra for dusting

1 tsp salt

1½ tsp active dry yeast

1 tbsp vegetable oil, plus extra for oiling

Grease a 9 x 5 x 3-inch/23 x 13 x 8-cm loaf pan. Sift the flour and salt together into a large warmed bowl. Stir in the yeast. Make a well in the center. Add the oil and water to the well and mix to form a soft dough. Turn out the dough onto a lightly floured counter and knead for 5–10 minutes, or until smooth and elastic. Put the dough in an oiled bowl, cover with plastic wrap, and let rise in a warm place for 1 hour, or until doubled in size.

Preheat the oven to 450°F/230°C.

Turn out the dough again and knead lightly. Shape into a rectangle the length of the pan and 3 times the width. With the long sides facing you, fold the top one-third down to cover the middle third, then fold the bottom one-third up and over the top and press together. Transfer to the prepared pan, seam-side down.

Bake in the center of the preheated oven for 25–30 minutes, or until it sounds hollow when tapped on the bottom. If the top is browning too much, reduce the temperature a little.

Transfer to a wire rack and let cool. Eat as fresh as possible.

Mixed seed bread

Makes 1 loaf

butter, for greasing

generous 2⅓ cups white bread flour, plus extra for dusting

scant 1 cup rye flour

1½ tsp salt

1 tsp active dry yeast

1 tbsp light brown sugar

1½ tbsp skim milk powder

1 tsp caraway seeds

½ tsp poppy seeds

½ tsp sesame seeds

1¼ cups lukewarm water

1½ tbsp sunflower oil, plus extra for oiling

2 tsp lemon juice

Topping

1 egg white

1 tbsp water

Grease a 9 x 5 x 3-inch/23 x 13 x 8-cm loaf pan. Sift the flours and salt together into a large warmed bowl. Stir in the yeast, sugar, milk powder, and seeds. Make a well in the center. Mix the water, oil, and lemon juice together and add to the well. Mix to form a dough.

Turn out the dough onto a lightly floured counter and knead for 5–10 minutes, or until smooth and elastic. Put the dough into an oiled bowl, cover with plastic wrap, and let rise in a warm place for 1 hour, or until doubled in size.

Turn out the dough again and knead lightly. Shape into a loaf and transfer to the prepared pan. Cover and let prove in a warm place for 30 minutes. Preheat the oven to 425°F/220°C.

To make the topping, lightly beat the egg white with the water. Brush over the top of the loaf, then gently press the seeds all over the top. Bake in the preheated oven for 25–30 minutes, or until it sounds hollow when tapped on the bottom. Transfer to a wire rack and let cool.

My special recipes

Notes ....

....

....

....

....

....

....

....

....

....

....

....

....

Notes ....

....

....

....

....

My special recipes

....
....
....
....
....
....
....
....
....
....
....
....
....
....

Notes ....
....
....
....
....

My special recipes

....
....
....
....
....
....
....
....
....
....
....
....
....

Notes ....

....
....
....
....

My special recipes

....

....

....

....

....

....

....

....

....

....

....

....

....

....

Notes ....

....

....

....

....

My special recipes

....

....

....

....

....

....

....

....

....

....

....

....

....

....

....

....

Notes ....

....

....

....

....

My special recipes

....
....
....
....
....
....
....
....
....
....
....
....
....
....

Notes ....
....
....
....
....

index

index

index